KNOW YOUR SUPREME RICHNESS

*The Absolute Non Dual teachings
Straight from the Source*

*This book is for every sincere seeker to know
The Eternal Truth beyond Birth and Death*

GM

INDIA • SINGAPORE • MALAYSIA

ISBN 979-8-88833-385-3

CONTENTS

Chapter II: GM's Questions and Answers 45

PREFACE

The Entire humanity is suffering through the personality, not knowing its immense beauty beyond dualities.

To make them aware that 'You Are Already That Supreme!' these teachings are the need of the hour.

To share the Truth about the Absolute, these Non Dual teachings by 'GM' are compiled and shared here!

GM says that Nobody Never Born, Nobody Dies! Then what are we exactly?

To know, whether we are awake or asleep or yet to awake... these teachings will be of immense help to every sincere seeker around the globe.

GM says,

"You are the Absolute already!

You prevail prior to Consciousness!

You are in your Supreme state already!

Yet you miss your True nature here...

By not knowing what you are exactly!"

To know how you miss your Supreme Reality upon the arrival of Consciousness...

GM's teachings simply wakes up your Consciousness within just now!

The purpose of this Book is only to make you aware of your Supreme Richness Just Now!

In what way does this teaching differ from others?

GM talks only on Consciousness and its nature and how this Consciousness is missing itself by not knowing itself as well why it should know itself and how it completes its journey by knowing its Source and becomes wholeness! Certainly, these teachings by GM are a milestone now, in this fast moving world where all run without knowing what we are...

Is this teaching very tough or Easy?

This is the easiest teaching possible as we need not go anywhere in search of the Truth within Just Now!

You need not move out anywhere to know the Truth!

You need not spend money to know the Truth.

Truth is not outside but within Just Now.

Just closing eyes is enough to know your Supreme Truth within.

These teachings are of immense use to every sincere seeker to enter inwardly!

ABOUT GM

'Nobody Never Born! Nobody dies!
You are already in your Supreme Reality!
Yet to Realize!'

...gm...

GM is a Self-Realized Master living in Chennai (Tamil Nadu), India. GM lives a simple life, and remains unknown to many. GM began her career as a scientist in the late 1980's.

GM transcended the duality in the late 2000's. Later, GM quit her job and remained in silence for several years. In the mid 2010's GM began teaching to a few sincere seekers who are dedicated to their own selves to Realize the Ultimate Reality.

GM's teachings are profound and awakening. It is quite rare to find a Master who has transcended Birth and Death. GM teachings are only of Consciousness and its nature. GM says whatever perceived here in space is nothing but a dream – Unreal! The teachings are free for any sincere seeker.

As GM teachings are totally awakening, they are compiled and shared here.

To know how you miss your Supreme Reality upon the arrival of Consciousness, GM's teachings are of immense help to wake up your Consciousness within Just Now!

The purpose of this book is only to make you aware of your Supreme Richness Just Now! Unlike many who talks only on body and mind...GM talks only on Consciousness...This is a very rare teaching as of now.

Chapter I

TEACHINGS OF GM

I, THE ABSOLUTE PREVAIL FOREVER!

I AM THE SOURCE OF ALL!

I AM EVER PRESENT!

I HAVE NO BEGINNING AND NO ENDING...

I AM FORMLESS, NAMELESS AND ATTRIBUTELESS!

I AM UNCHANGING, UNMOVING, EVER PRESENT!

I AM TOTALLY INDEPENDENT!

I AM THE SOURCE OF CONSCIOUSNESS!

CONSCIOUSNESS ARISES OUT OF ME!

AND MERGES BACK IN ME!

NOTHING NEVER HAPPENS TO ME!

I AM ALWAYS IN MY ORIGINAL SUPREME STATE!

I AM BEYOND BIRTH AND DEATH!

I AM ALREADY COMPLETE AND TOTAL!

I AM THE WHOLENESS!

I KNOW THE PLAY BY CONSCIOUSNESS!

I REMAIN UNBOTHERED ABOUT ALL THE PLAY HAPPENINGS...

AS I KNOW THEY ARE NOT REAL!

I AM THE SOURCE OF ALL!

...GM...

1. JUST NOW YOU ARE THAT!

Just Now You Are That!

Your Consciousness has to know its Source.

But still it is trapped by the personality and added labels and refuses to remain Conscious of itself.

Once your Consciousness is Conscious of itself, it starts waking up from the dream and knows its Original Supreme Richness...

And declares that "It is never born... But ever present".

2. YOU ARE EVER PRESENT HERE!

You are That!

Whenever you remain bothered whether it is a waking state or a dream state...

It shows that you are yet to know...

What this Consciousness is......

Which plays the trick and makes you believe all is real!

It is better that your Consciousness wakes up at the earliest and knows its immense beauty beyond boundaries.

Till you wake up from the dream by Consciousness, you are stuck at the form level and remain disturbed only.

Nothing never happens Here!

You are already in your Supreme Richness!

Whatever that happens within space is by Consciousness only!

You are beyond Consciousness Just Now!

Just Observe silently, wake up and Know.........

Whether forms are real!

You are more than the form, Just Now!

You have no boundary!

You are infinite!

See how you are caught by the dream called form?

Close your eyes...

Know your unlimited potential!

You are ever present here!

3. CONSCIOUSNESS AND THE FORM!

The form is only a Conscious form!

It is only Consciousness that functions through the form!

The form appears only due to Consciousness!

Form cannot happen but for Consciousness!

Each and every cell of the form is by Consciousness itself!

Form and Consciousness are not separate.

In your Consciousness only form happens... Just Now!

First, you are Conscious of yourself as 'I am ness' without words.

In your 'I am ness' Consciousness only... form appears... now!

Instead of focusing attention on your 'I am ness'... your Consciousness is trapped by accepting that it is a form only and never knows that it is prior to form.

By accepting the form as itself...not knowing that it is only using the form...

Your Consciousness is continuously trapped at the form level identity.

Dream happens only at the form level!

Once your Consciousness is Conscious of itself and starts knowing the stillness within...then it starts waking up from the form level dream...!

Only upon waking up totally from the form level Identity......

Your Consciousness knows that it is never born and ever present!

The form by Consciousness is useful not only to know your existence as 'I am ness'... But also to know what you are exactly... i.e... The Wholeness, the Ultimate Reality beyond duality... Just Now!

4. "I AMNESS" CONSCIOUSNESS

Every knowing is by Consciousness itself!

Every form is by Consciousness itself!

Entire manifestation is by Consciousness itself!

The whole functioning of this entire manifestation is by Consciousness itself!

Every living being is by Consciousness itself!

Every atom...sub atom... object perceived is by Consciousness itself!

The entire space is by Consciousness itself!

Whatever that appears, functions, moves in space are also by Consciousness itself!

Entire universe, cosmos, galaxies, world are also by Consciousness itself!

Space, air, fire, water and earth are also by Consciousness itself!

There is nothing here other than Consciousness. This Consciousness is universal!

There is never any person! All forms are only Conscious forms!

This Consciousness is nothing but your 'I am ness' Consciousness... In your 'I am ness' only everything appears...moves...and disappears...

This you never know...as you are trapped by the personality imposed on you...unknowingly!

Whatever you see, hear and know... Where else it is happening?

Can anything be known without this Consciousness?

When you are Conscious, you get to know everything...

When this Consciousness is absent, how can you know anything?

So understand first...

It is your 'I am ness' Consciousness which is the base for everything that appears or happens...

Now, tell me...

WHO IS DOING WHAT?

First know! Only in your 'I am ness' Consciousness everything is happening!

All actions are by Consciousness itself.

Every movement is by Consciousness itself!

Only unmoving, unchanging Absolute is ever present here!

Consciousness happens for a shorter duration and the play happens.

You are not the play!

You are the Observer of the play by Consciousness right now!

You, the Observer, Prevail Forever!

Your presence is throughout...!

Know the joy which is endless...

Whether Consciousness happens or not...

You the Absolute Prevail here forever...!

What more you want?

I am telling you that you are the Ultimate already!

There is nothing greater than you!

There is no Truth other than you!

What more you want?

Entire humanity is like this.........

As they do not know what this Consciousness is which plays the trick and makes you believe all is real!

Nobody never born!

Consciousness identifies itself as a person with a specific shape and design unknowingly!

What is a form?

Can there be any form without your Consciousness?

It is your Consciousness which creates forms and functions through the forms and drops forms too...

Consciousness is Ever Here! Consciousness is universal.

Now by identifying itself as a person, it first accepts that it is born and now accepts death also as real...not knowing that it prevails already prior to form.

Consciousness is more than the form.

How can it die?

Only forms disappear but Consciousness functioning within all forms is ever here.

Your Consciousness trapped by the personality should know that it is Consciousness only and not the form... which happens for a shorter duration.

There is not even an iota of Truth in whatever that is perceived within space.

Truth is within.

Truth cannot die!

That which disappears cannot be the Truth.

Once this is understood deeply... then Consciousness will not search anything outside and spend time uselessly.

Rather it goes inward deeply... through stillness and starts knowing itself.

Whatever perceived in space is constantly changing.

What Truth are you searching within space as everything changes at a greater speed in no time?

Consciousness is unnecessarily spending time outside as it takes all to be real.

There is no remedy for this sickness as all that appear, disappear too.

Why? Because, they are nothing but the reflections only and not real!

All your worries are only about a film that is perceived in the screen of spacc.

Can a film be real?

Is it not a reflection of light projected over the screen?

There is only one medicine...that is your Consciousness within... should know that it is only Consciousness and using the form.

Your Consciousness only uses the form but it is more than the form.

Your Consciousness within which is stillness... beyond words...contains the seed of the entire manifestation.

Without your Consciousness there is neither the world nor any manifestation.

Know your immense beauty beyond limitations...!

Know your Highest potential beyond Birth and Death!

First know... whatever that happens within Conscious field are not you!

You, the Observer, Prevail Forever!

Nothing has never happened to you!

Whatever appears to happen is like a dream happening, not real...

Having known this, can your Consciousness remain worried?

You are enough unto yourself! Because your Self contains all...!

Know your Supreme Richness! Just Now!

5. JUST A PLAY OF ELEMENTS ONLY!

Whatever appearances that happen in a waking state or a dream state are nothing but a play of elements!

Spontaneously elements interact and forms are created.

Whether it is a dream in sleep or waking state, all that appears are nothing but a play of elements by Consciousness itself!

The mind does not exist!

That does not exist... cannot create too...!

Entire creations......

Both living and non living within space are by Consciousness itself...!

Your 'I am ness' Consciousness only creates spontaneously.

In your 'I am ness' only just now forms are created!

What is a form?

Is it not made up of elements?

Where does element happen?

Is it not in your Consciousness?

Just Now in your Consciousness only... entire manifestation happens!

If you are not Conscious, where is any form? Or any manifested object...?

First, you are Conscious of 'yourself '.!

In your Consciousness, entire manifestation happens simultaneously!

Your Consciousness and the world, cosmos, universe and all forms are not separate.

Without Consciousness, nothing is created here!

Consciousness is the base of all creations...

Nature of Consciousness itself is creation only.

Consciousness creates space, air, fire, water and earth spontaneously.

Every form that appears too is created by Consciousness itself!

All Elements are also by Consciousness only!

Only elements interact with various combinations of permutations and forms of various shapes are created Just Now...!

Light is Consciousness!

But for light, there is neither the element nor any forms... with different shapes...

Just Now in your light of Consciousness only... all forms appear, function and disappear too...

Similarly, in your sleep, a small of ray of light happens spontaneously and forms are created which you call as a dream.

The mind does not exist!

Only thoughts appear to disappear! Where?

In your Consciousness only!

Entire creation is by the spontaneous play of elements in Consciousness...

Whether it is a dream state or waking state...

Know this!

Know you never do anything!

All by Consciousness itself!

You only Observe! Just Now!

You are always the Observer of Consciousness and its contents.

The Observer remains unbothered about the perceived!

You are That!

Whenever you remain bothered whether it is a waking state or a dream state...

It shows that you are yet to know...

What this Consciousness is...which plays the trick and makes you believe all are real!

It is better that your Consciousness wakes up at the earliest and knows its immense beauty beyond boundaries.

Till you wake up from the dream by Consciousness, you are stuck at the form level and remain disturbed only.

Nothing Never Happens Here!

You are already in your Supreme Richness!

Whatever that happens within space is by Consciousness only.

You are beyond Consciousness Just Now!

Just Observe silently...! Wake up!

Know! Whether forms are real!

You are more than the form...just now!

You have no boundary......

You are infinite!

See how you are caught by the dream called form?

Close your eyes...

Know your unlimited potential!

You are ever present here!

6. JUST NOW!

Space is created by your Consciousness only Just Now!

Entire manifestation is happening in your 'I am ness' only Just Now!

Total functioning of the entire manifestation is by your Consciousness only...

Just Now!

Whatever perceived within space is nothing but the reflections of the light within!

Light is Consciousness!

Out of light... the entire manifestation happens within space Just Now!

Can there be a world or your form without your Consciousness?

Only in your Consciousness... your form and the world happen... Just Now!

Know the immense beauty of your 'I am ness'!

7. YOU DO NOTHING!

You never do anything.!

All by Consciousness itself...!

You only Observe!

You do nothing...

Breathing, heartbeat, blood circulation, enzymatic reactions, metabolic activities needed for the survival of the form are spontaneously done by Consciousness!

Do you make any effort?

Sunrise, sunset, rain, and entire manifestations and their total functioning are also spontaneous by Consciousness.

The very base for knowing your existence...

'I am ness' also happens by Consciousness itself!

Have you started your Consciousness?

It just happens...!

Throughout the waking state......

Consciousness functions... through all forms and makes you believe all is real.

Consciousness disappears when sleep happens!

Do you make any effort?

Right from the beginning of the waking state, till the beginning of sleep...

Entire manifestation, functioning and all movements are by Consciousness only.

So all by Consciousness itself!

Consciousness functions through forms.

Never any person here!

So all by Consciousness itself...!

Then who is the Observer of all that happen?

YOU ARE THAT!

Now do you accept that you never do anything?

You only Observe!

Consciousness arises out of Awareness and merges back in Awareness only!

Consciousness is dependent on Awareness.

Consciousness creates forms and comes to know its existence only through the form.

Unknowingly... it identifies itself as a form though it is prior to form.

By accepting the form as itself......

It accepts the Birth and Death as real... unknowingly.

Once it meets a Realized, it comes to know that it is Consciousness only and not the form.

Then it starts remaining Conscious of itself and knows its Eternity beyond Birth and Death!

It finds its Source...once it abides in stillness.

Hence abiding in stillness is the most essential.

8. KNOW YOUR IMMENSE BEAUTY!

When Your Consciousness identifies itself as a tiny form with a fixed label, it accepts that it is separate from the world unknowingly!

Once your Consciousness is Conscious of itself, it starts knowing the stillness within and knows that the entire world is within Consciousness.

See the contradiction:

Consciousness unknowingly accepts that it is separate from the world at the form level!

Once it is known that it is only Consciousness... Then it knows the entire manifestation as world, cosmos, universe are by Consciousness itself.

Now it knows that nothing is separate from itself.

Now, tell me...

Is it not necessary to know that you are Conscious only at present without which nothing is here?

Your Consciousness is the lively principle functioning through all forms.

Know your Immense Beauty Beyond Limitations!

First, it accepts the form as itself unknowingly!

After meeting a Realized... it knows that it is Consciousness only at present.

It is only Consciousness within the form which knows its Ultimate Source...!

When Consciousness is stuck at the form level, it cannot know its Ultimate Source!

Remain Conscious and know!

9. YOUR SELF CONTAINS ALL!

Your Self contains all...!

You are infinite already!

But you accept yourself as a finite form.

By accepting the finite form as yourself you see the other forms are separate from you.

You never knew that all forms are by Consciousness itself.

All forms are Conscious forms only.

They all happen in your 'I am ness' only.

Whatever that appears in your 'I am ness' are yourself only!

Nothing is separate from your Self...!

Your Self contains all...!

First, know this!

10. YOU ARE BEYOND ENLIGHTENMENT!

Enlightenment itself is a Dream!

The Observer is prior to Dream!

Nothing never happens to the Observer!

And you are That!

Consciousness has to transcend itself totally to know that it is beyond dream!

The Observer is prior to Dream!

Even enlightenment itself is a Dream only!

Nothing never happens to the Observer!

Don't get caught by these fancy words enlightenment... ecstasy...etc...,

Your Consciousness has to wake up totally... to know its Wholeness!

Your Consciousness realizes its unborn nature beyond dualities and knows that it is never born!

Whatever born is only a dream... not real!

You, the Absolute are Non Dual...!

Whatever that happens in duality is never you!

You only Observe Just Now!

11. BE YOURSELF!

Be yourself!

This is totally misunderstood. It means... Be Conscious of Yourself!

Know your Conscious presence without words.

Know! Your Self Contains all.!

Your Self is prior to World, Cosmos and Entire Creations.

You know the stillness within. This is the beginning of your Consciousness.

This Stillness contains all...!

When you abide in stillness... you know the Peace and Joy within.

When you are Conscious of yourself, your Consciousness starts waking up...from the dream... called manifestations.

But this statement is totally misunderstood at the personality level.

Your Consciousness is identifying itself as a personality unknowingly.

It accepts itself as a form with certain imposed labels as itself and considers itself as a personality only... till it meets a Realized.

Only a Realized says that you are Conscious only at present and not the labels added.

Then your Consciousness remains Conscious of itself, starts waking up...Consciously and knows its Highest potential beyond Birth and Death.

Be yourself does not indicate that you remain as a personality.

It means...Be Conscious of Yourself!

Unless you are Conscious and abide in stillness consistently...

You cannot know your Supreme Richness!

12. LOVE THYSELF!

Consciousness is love!

Love is universal!

Entire universe functions out of love.

The entire space is filled with love!

River, mountain, trees, flowers, sun, stars, moon, etc., all function out of love!

Love does not expect anything! It simply functions out of joy!

Entire manifestation happens out of love by Consciousness!

Consciousness creates all creatures out of love and functions through all out of love! This love is infinite and unending...

There are never any persons!

All by Consciousness itself!

When there is no person who is loving whom?

Only Consciousness appears as all and functions through all!

Love is bubbling throughout space!

Flower blossoming...River running...Birds chirping...

All by Consciousness itself...out of love!

Love Thyself!

Once Consciousness starts loving itself... it focuses attention on itself and gets to know... its immense potential within.

You are enough unto yourself!

Your Consciousness is more than enough for you to know your Supreme Richness!

13. ONLY A REALIZED CAN WAKE UP YOUR CONSCIOUSNESS!

It is always Consciousness here appearing as so many forms!

Through certain forms it gets to know its Supreme Reality.

Mostly Consciousness is deep asleep by taking itself to be a finite form with fixed labels.

Unless it comes across a Realized... it never wakes up.!

Consciousness is conditioning itself as a form... and its story goes on... at the personality level. It never knows that it is only Consciousness.

It never knows that it is Consciousness only out of which world, cosmos and all forms happen. Its infinite potential remains unknown to itself.

It never knows that it is beyond form... and all forms happen out of it.

It never knows its unborn nature... so it accepts the birth as real.

It never knows its deathlessness... hence constant fear of losing the form.

It accepts all happenings as real though all are unreal!

It never wakes up from its unreal dream... till it meets a Realized.

Only a Realized can wake up your Consciousness!

Only Consciousness which is brighter comes nearer to the Realized and starts listening.

Consciousness which is very dull and sleeping cannot understand the words by the Realized... as it is more into asleep.

That which comes nearer to a Realized is more blessed to receive the teachings directly from the Realized.

That which listens, abides and wakes up...from the Unreal dream Consciously... is the most blessed as it knows its Eternity forever!

Chapter II

GM'S
QUESTIONS AND ANSWERS

1. I AM TOTAL, COMPLETE AND PERFECT ALREADY

Q: Dear GM, what is Non dual? In what way this Non dual teaching helps me?

GM:

I, the Absolute alone prevail here forever!

I am Unchanging, Unmoving and Ever present!

I am Total, Complete and Perfect already!

I am indescribable, beyond words...

I am unmoving, beyond all movements!

I am Ever in My Eternity Beyond Birth and Death!

I am beyond duality.

I am the Source of innumerable lights of lights... indescribable...

I am the Source of light itself!

Nothing never happens to Me!

I am Non Dual!

Spontaneously, a speck of light arises out of Me as Consciousness and it knows its presence as 'I am ness' through the form created in space just now!

Here with this arrival of 'I am ness'... Duality begins!

With the beginning of this 'I am ness' entire manifestation happens including universe, cosmos, world and all forms!

This Consciousness knowing itself as 'I am' through the form now starts identifying itself as a form though it is prior to form just now...

By accepting itself as a form Consciousness accepts that it is born and has a constant fear of death too...

Now this Consciousness is trapped by the personality with imposed labels and accepts all to be real.

Consciousness happens out of Me!

The play at the form level goes on within space by Consciousness itself... right from waking till sleep happens.

Consciousness never knows that the entire manifestation arises out of it...! (Speck of light)......

Not knowing that whatever perceived in space are only its own reflection as objects!

Since Consciousness does not know that it is light only right now, it accepts the entire reflections in space as real... till it meets a Realized who has known what this Consciousness is and who knows the Source of Consciousness is Awareness!

It is stumbling at the form level (duality).

Question: 'In what way this Non dual teaching helps me?'

Though you are non dual right now...

You are asking this question at the duality level as you are yet to know that you are non dual, unborn!

I, the Absolute (Non Dual) now using this Conscious form (dual) and answering your question.

I am the Source of Consciousness!

I am prior to Consciousness!

I know what this Consciousness is!

I know this Consciousness arises out of Me!

And merges back in Me!

I know the entire play happenings within conscious field in space are just a play only... not real!

But your Consciousness is yet to know what it is... as it is trapped by the personality accepting itself as a tiny form with fixed labels imposed.

I am Non Dual!

I know what this Consciousness is...

As I remain the Source of Consciousness always!

You are dual, just now at the Conscious level as your Consciousness is yet to know Me (The Absolute, Awareness)! To Me, nothing is happening here!

To you, every happening is real!

To Me, there is neither birth nor death!

To you, birth and death are more real!

I am prior to waking, dream, sleep states!

I remain untouched by all these states!

To you... waking, dreaming and sleeping all appear real... as you are yet to know the Observer in you!

I, the Observer, prevail here forever!

I silently Observe the entire film happening in Conscious field and remain unaffected.

You are yet to know the Observer (Me, The Absolute).

Hence you remain affected by the entire happenings taking all to be real and remain struggling...

I, the Absolute, now use this Conscious form and teach you that

'You are Never Born, You Never Die!

You are Eternal!

You are the Supreme!

Whatever perceived in space is only a dream... not real...!

Go inward!

And know the peace within!

Through peace you know Me!

By knowing what your Consciousness is, you know Me!

(The Absolute, The Wholeness)

By knowing Me (The Source) your Consciousness knows its Wholeness!

And knows its Eternity beyond birth and death'!

Now, tell me is it not more essential to listen to my teachings to know that you are non dual only and not the dual?

I am the Source of Consciousness.!
Consciousness happens out of Me.!

Q: *Beloved GM, Why I want to know myself?*

GM:

Certainly this question is by Consciousness itself.

Know!

Your Consciousness comes to know its presence spontaneously only by morning 5 or so and functions till sleep happens. Your Consciousness creates all forms through the elemental interaction spontaneously.

Unknowingly your Consciousness accepts itself as born and receives all concepts imposed on it as Real and lives with a constant fear of death as it has accepted that it is born.

Your Consciousness remains incomplete and restless throughout the waking state accepting all happenings as Real.

It does not know that whatever it perceives is like a dream.

Consciousness does not know that it is only a dream which is perceived as Real.

Hence it struggles to find out the solution then and there for every conflict.

What will be the remedy for your dream?

You are lying down in your bed. In your sleep dream you feel thirsty but don't get water.

You move here and there in search of water and remain restless.

Once you are awake you know that it is your dream only... not Real and feel relieved.

Similarly now in waking state you take all happenings as Real and seek remedy not knowing that this waking state itself is a bigger dream. The only solution for every conflict in this waking state is the awakening of your Consciousness which is not Conscious of itself and unaware of its True Nature.

Once Consciousness knows itself, it knows its Unborn, Eternal, Supreme Reality and says it is Never Born.

Know how your Consciousness is unknowingly caught by its own dream not knowing its Unborn Supreme Ultimate Reality. Consciousness should know that whatever happens within space is exactly a dream... not Real but appears as Real.

In your sleep dream so many forms appear and function.

Once the dream is over, where are they?

Similarly, now in your dreamy Consciousness, the total functioning of the entire manifestation makes you believe all happenings as Real.

Once Consciousness is awakened there is neither the manifestation nor any forms......

You know that you are the Ultimate!

Consciousness is neither born nor dies!

It lives throughout...its potential remains... Forever...!

Only forms appear and disappear in Consciousness.

As long as Consciousness is limiting itself as a tiny figure with a certain identity, it remains incomplete.

Rather it should know that it is Consciousness only and starts remaining Conscious to find out its Source which is within.

Then it is complete!

When Consciousness is Conscious of itself, it is Awareness!

Awareness is Complete, Total and Perfect...!

Consciousness remains incomplete till it knows its Source which is Awareness.

Now, you know why you want to know yourself?

Is it not?

Go through this answer deeply...

Once you understand what is said above, you will never miss knowing yourself.

The Observer remains unconcerned

About that which appear and disappear

As they are not Real...!

Q: Beloved GM, What is the nature of this Consciousness, why does this Consciousness disappear in my deep sleep?

GM:

The nature of Consciousness is Creativity...

The entire manifestation is created by your 'I am ness' Consciousness only...

Consciousness is everywhere ...

It is infinite...

It knows its presence only through a physical matrix.

Hence it creates the form and knows itself as 'I am ness'.

It is Consciousness functioning through the forms...

But for Consciousness, neither forms nor any manifested objects within space Just Now!

It knows its presence as 'I am ness' through the form.

Elements interact and forms are created simultaneously with the knowing 'I am ness'.

Universal Consciousness now knows its presence as 'I am ness' within a form.

It starts identifying itself as a finite form as it knows its presence only through the form.

It never knows that it is prior to form.

In deep sleep, you do not know that you exist.

You come to know your existence only upon the arrival of Consciousness as 'I am ness'.

But for the elemental interactions 'I am ness' cannot happen.

Elements do not know when they interact.

Consciousness does not know when it happens.

Elemental interactions and 'I am ness' Consciousness happening are spontaneous...

With the arrival of 'I am ness', the world and the entire manifestations happen simultaneously...

Spontaneously elements interact... Just Now!

Spontaneously 'I am ness' happens... Just Now!

Spontaneously the world, Cosmos, the entire manifestations happen...

Just Now!

Here everything is spontaneous!

Entire spontaneous activity is by Consciousness itself...!

There are never any persons…!

You are asking, why this Consciousness disappears in deep sleep?

'I am ness' Consciousness appears due to spontaneous elemental interactions and the world appears in your 'I am ness'.

Your Conscious presence is known only at a particular temperature.

When elements interaction is at the lesser level, metabolic activity is also at the lesser level.

At a particular temperature, your body is frozen and 'I am ness' is not known which you call as sleep.

Sleep is also a spontaneous happening only.

So, the arrival of 'I am ness' and the disappearance of 'I am ness' depend upon the elemental interaction only.

The world depends upon your 'I am ness'.

'I am ness' depends upon elements!

So the entire play happening within space is by the elemental interactions only.

But "You, the Observer Prevail prior to waking, dream and sleep states and have nothing to do with the elemental play!"

You are prior to Dream,

Form, Space and Consciousness...!

...gm...

Q: *Beloved GM, Can you explain, 'Who am I'?*

GM:

You are The Ultimate Supreme!

You Never Born, Never Die!

You are ever present here!

You are The Absolute Just Now! Yet to know...!

Nothing never happens to you!

You are in your Original Supreme state already!

Still how you are asking now, 'Who am I'?

This question happens as you are yet to know your Supreme Richness!

Now you are Conscious of yourself!

Is it not?

Otherwise, this question cannot happen.

But your 'I am ness' Consciousness is trapped by the personality identity...

So it is asking 'who am I ?' Unknowingly!

First your Consciousness which is conditioning itself as a person should remain free from the imposed conditions and know that it is Consciousness only at present!

By accepting itself as the personality, it accepts Birth and Death as Real and struggles throughout... not knowing that it is Consciousness only in which the form happens... Just Now!

Basically, this question is by Consciousness as it is accepting itself as a tiny form with imposed labels...

Consciousness is beyond identification.

But it accepts all that is perceived in space as real as it is yet to know itself!

The first step is this 'I am ness' Consciousness has to know that it is Consciousness only at present.

This can be known by closing eyes and knowing the stillness within.

In this stillness, Consciousness knows its presence and knows that it is beyond boundaries and all forms perceived in space.

By knowing the stillness within, your Consciousness comes to know that it is prior to form...prior to space and prior to the entire manifestation within space!

Now Consciousness knows that it is prior to all movements in space.

Every movement happens only by Consciousness within!

First your 'I am ness' Consciousness comes to know that it is Consciousness only at present.

This is only the first step towards knowing its Wholeness, the Ultimate Reality beyond dualities.

Now your Consciousness which happens for a shorter duration say morning 5 am or so till night 10 pm or so should know from where it arises and where it merges back... that is... its Source must be known...

Then only it remains complete.

First Consciousness comes to know that 'I am ness' is only Consciousness and not a person.

This knowing Consciousness as Consciousness is only a beginning...

This knowing is not final...!

Now this 'I am ness' Consciousness abides in stillness constantly and transcends itself and knows its Source of Awareness...

Once it transcends itself... it knows that it is The Absolute already!

Nothing never happens to it!

It knows that it is Never Born...!

Where is the death for the one That which is Never Born?

It knows that it is ever present here!

It knows whatever that happen within Conscious field in space are only a dream happening...... not Real!

Now it is awakened totally and knows that it is The Ultimate beyond dualities...

Non Dual...

'Who am I'? Question is at the personality level by Consciousness.

Once Consciousness knows that it is Consciousness only...then it is free from all that Perceived in space...as it starts waking up inwardly by stabilizing in its Source constantly...

Finally, Consciousness knows that it is The Absolute!

Non Dual...

Consciousness is the only key to the door of the Supreme!

Of course, there is no door! Supreme is Ever Here Just Now!

Consciousness locks itself through the personality and remains unknown to itself...!

Once Consciousness is Conscious of itself, it unlocks itself from the conditioned identities and remains open.

By remaining Conscious consistently, it transcends itself and knows its Supreme Reality!

Use this key Consciousness by remaining Conscious of yourself...!

Abide in stillness constantly...!

Your Consciousness will wake up from its manifested dream Consciously and knows its Eternal, unlimited potential, Ever Here as the Absolute!

All that you need to find out 'who you are'... is to use the key viz... Consciousness constantly...

My teachings are of immense help to your Consciousness to wake up at the earliest to know 'What you are exactly'! Just Now!

All that needed is to wake up from the personality identity first...

Then know you are Consciousness only... at present...

And finally, your Consciousness knows its Eternal Source beyond dualities.

You are the Observer only!

Never the Observed!

The Observer is Never Born!

Non Dual!

The Observer is ever present!

You are That!

All happenings are Spontaneous.!
None of the happenings are Real.!

...gm...

Q: *Beloved GM...you say 'the Observer is not the Observed!'... can you explain on this?*

GM:

You take the Observer to be the Observed...that is why you need explanation for this.

What is Observed here in space?

Just appearances and their movements... Only!

From where do they all appear Just Now?

In your 'I am ness' Consciousness only!

But for your Consciousness neither the space nor any objects here in space!

In your 'I am ness' Consciousness only everything happens now!

When your Consciousness disappears in sleep there is neither the world nor any manifestations here!

So where do all appear...Just Now?

They all appear... not somewhere... but in your Consciousness... Just Now!

This point should be noted deeply... Otherwise, you will miss the essence of my teachings!

Whatever Observed are only from your 'I am ness' Consciousness Just Now!

Your 'I am ness' happens spontaneously by morning 5 or so and you know that you exist... not earlier in sleep.

Your existence is known through 'I am ness'... Simultaneously the world happens in your 'I am ness' only.

All that Observed in space is by your Consciousness only...!

My question is:

Are all that appear in space remain permanent?

Where do they all go... once you are no more Conscious of yourself?

Are not all that Observed in space depend on your Consciousness?

When your 'I am ness' Consciousness itself is known only for a shorter duration say from morning 5 or so till sleep happens..........

Your 'I am ness' and its manifested objects appear in your waking state and disappear in your sleep state......

Then, this 'I am ness' which appears and disappears... only displays whatever that appear in space as the world, cosmos etc.,

Can that which appear and disappear be Real...?

When all that Observed are not Real...

What is Real here in space?

Who is the Observer of all that appear and disappear?

Why don't you find out the Observer in you right now?

And know you are only the Observer and not the Observed...!

My question is who is the Observer of all that Observed?

Your Consciousness is trapped by the personality unknowingly and never knows that it is Consciousness only at present.

Your Consciousness identifies itself as a form and accepts... all that perceived in space as Real... till it knows itself!

Your Consciousness is trapped at the form level... never knowing all that perceived is only a dream happening and not Real...!

There is no remedy at the form level identity...!

Your Consciousness should know that it is Consciousness only through stillness.

Then it knows all that perceived in space as objects are nothing but the reflections of light within!

It is only the Light... Reflected in space as all objects perceived now!

There is no Reality in whatever perceived in space like the dream objects.

Then your Consciousness stops giving Reality to all that perceived in space and transcends itself totally into its Source of Awareness and knows the Wholeness...that it is The Observer only and remains unbothered about all the play happenings in space as they are nothing but an Unreal dream!

By knowing its Wholeness, it knows that it is the ever present Observer only!

It has nothing to do with the Observed contents in space as it knows its beyondness prior to Birth and Death duality...!

The Observer is Non Dual!

The Observer is Never Born!

Ever present!

The Observer is the Source of Consciousness!

Only a film play is going on in the screen of space by Consciousness spontaneously......as the world, cosmos, all appearances...and none of the scenes are Real...!

All the time your Consciousness which was sleeping conveniently at the form level identity taking the dream objects to be more Real......

Now wakes up by abiding in stillness consistently and transcends itself beyond space and knows that it is only the Observer prior to all the dream happenings in space and nothing has never happened to the Observer!

The Observer is ever present prior to space!

All that appear to happen in space are not Real and only a dream...

Never Real...!

Now tell me,

How you the Observer prior to Consciousness get caught by the play and identify yourself as the object to say that the Observer is the Observed?

Your Consciousness has to know what it is exactly... as it is yet to wake up!

Till it knows its Source...The Wholeness......

It is trapped by the dream play consistently...!

Better wake up Consciously and

Know your Wholeness beyond duality...

Know you are only the Observer right now...!

Nothing has never happened to you...!

You are already Total, Complete and Perfect!

You, the Observer alone Prevail here!

Know!

The Observer is prior to dream!

Whatever Observed are only a dream!

Now do you know...Why I say, 'The Observer is not the Observed...?'

Know the Real Within.!

Observe the Unreal outside.!

...gm...

2. ALL FORMS ARE CONSCIOUS FORMS

Q: Beloved GM, Though I am part of Universal Consciousness to Realize the Truth the worldly thoughts are barriers. Are the world and myself different?

GM:

Again you are blaming thoughts are preventing your Realization.

Where do thoughts exist?

Can they exist if you are not Conscious?

Instead of worrying about thoughts... worry about your Consciousness.

It will lead you to the Highest...!

Find out why this Consciousness has happened?

How this Consciousness has happened?

Investigate about yourself...!

Then all mysteries will be solved as all exist in your Consciousness only.

You are asking whether yourself and the world are different?

In your Consciousness only the world, cosmos and the entire manifestation happens.

Like sun and Sunrays, your Consciousness and the world are not separate.

Once you are Conscious, the world is there.

The world remains in your Consciousness as long as you are Conscious...disappears once your Consciousness disappears... as in deep sleep.

Why do you bother about the world which cannot remain without Consciousness?

Bother only about your Consciousness which happens for a shorter duration from morning till night up to sleep and find out what it is...!

Only the Dream begins from the space and ends up in space...!

You, the Observer prevail prior to space...!

...gm...

Q: Dear GM, Why Consciousness happens?

GM:

This you need to investigate.

This question is by Consciousness itself.

Universal Consciousness is always here but it knows its presence only through a physical form.

But for form it cannot know itself.

Form is essential for its knowing.

Spontaneously you become Conscious of your presence by early morning 5 or so and you remain Conscious till night up to sleep.

Spontaneously this form is created by the elemental interaction.

The indwelling principle is Consciousness as 'I am'.

This principle sustains the seed of the entire manifestation in nascent stage within.

Through form the seed manifests itself as the world, cosmos, universe etc., which you perceive in space.

Now the entire play happening in space is by the seed which is the result of the elemental interaction.

When elements interact, Conscious presence 'I am' is known through the form, simultaneously the world is also perceived as manifestation.

Now the Conscious presence 'I am' depends on the interaction of elements.

Elements do not know when they interact...Conscious presence 'I am' does not know when it appears as it is dependent on elements.

Entire manifestation depends upon this Conscious presence 'I am' as it sustains the seed within.

Now, understand clearly... all happen... spontaneously...!

Spontaneously elements interact, Conscious presence 'I am' is felt through the created form and the whole manifestation is created simultaneously.

All are simultaneous happenings...!

Entire play is out of ignorance only...!

Spontaneously, this ignorant play goes on......

As long as you are not aware of this Conscious play, you are continuously deceived by your own perception.

Once your Conscious is Conscious of itself then it starts knowing its Source and says, 'I am beyond Consciousness, I have nothing to do with Consciousness and its play' and you remain cool whether Consciousness happens or not...

as now you know about this spontaneous happenings of all is nothing... but a play and unreal.

So Consciousness knowing its Source is most important.

Till then such questions happen out of ignorance of the Self.

Infinite peace and endless joy are

Known throughout this inner journey...!

Q: *Beloved GM, I know that I have neither birth nor death. How to experience this? How to know my Supreme Reality? Can you explain?*

GM:

You are already the Supreme...beyond Birth and Death!

Nothing has never happened to you!

Now this question is at the form level by your Consciousness, as your Consciousness is yet to know that it is Never Born...!

You are asking how to experience this?

Certainly, you cannot experience it. Experiences are not you!

You prevail prior to all experiences!

Experiences are at the form level within space...

The Ultimate Truth is beyond form! Beyond space...!

It cannot be experienced.

This Ultimate Truth remains unknown to you as your 'I am ness' Consciousness is trapped at the personality level taking itself to be a form with imposed labels.

Once your Consciousness is Conscious of itself by abiding in stillness, beyond words...your Consciousness starts waking up...

Your Consciousness arises from Awareness and merges back in Awareness itself.

Awareness is the Source of your Consciousness...!

Your 'I am ness' Consciousness is the Source of the entire manifestation.

The entire manifestation is by your 'I am ness' Consciousness only... Just Now!

Having known this... you will not be trapped by the personality identification and very easily you can remain free from the personality level and remain Conscious of yourself!

How to remain Conscious of yourself?

Close your eyes!

You know that you exist without words. This knowing your presence without words is your 'I am ness' Consciousness at present.

This peace, stillness is only the beginning of your 'I am ness' Consciousness.

Once your Consciousness is Conscious of itself and abides constantly in stillness spontaneously your Consciousness transcends itself and knows its Wholeness!

To the Absolute, there is neither Birth nor Death!

The Absolute is Non Dual.

The Absolute is the Source of Consciousness!

By merging in Source constantly, your Consciousness, transcends itself and becomes the Source itself.......like a river merging in the ocean becomes the ocean itself!

The Source is Non Dual! You are already the Source only!

Yet to know it as your Consciousness is trapped at the personality level identities... unknowingly.

Better remain Conscious of yourself and know!

Consciousness is the only key to the door of Supreme!

Use the key and find out your Supreme Reality beyond Birth and Death!

Can you?

Your Consciousness prior to form, prior to space...

Now accepts itself as a form within space...!

Q: Beloved GM, To whom I belong to?

GM:

With what Identity you are asking this?

Certainly at the personality level only!

Are you a thing?

Do you ever know that you are not a thing?

But the source of all things!

Can this question be asked when you are not Conscious?

See how your Consciousness is conditioning itself as a thing, a form with limited shape and design and remains as a slave and asking, 'To whom I belong to...'?

What are you now?

Are you just a form?

Can your form function when you are not conscious?

How do you know that 'you exist'?

Can this form exist when you are not Conscious of yourself?

Do you know that principle by which you come to know that you exist?

Do you know that principle by which entire manifestations and all forms including your form happen just now?

Have you ever pondered on these questions?

You simply accept yourself as a tiny form with fixed labels and asking...

'To whom I belong to?'

What a pity?

Not knowing your presence...!

Your presence is known through 'I am ness'... Consciousness just now...

You know that 'you exist!'

But do not know, what 'you are!' exactly!

At present your 'I am ness' is Consciousness... only...

In your 'I am ness' Consciousness only you come to know that you exist!

In deep sleep you do not know that you exist!

Only upon the arrival of 'I am ness'... Consciousness you know your presence through the form...!

Your Consciousness is prior to form!

It has no boundary! It is Infinite...

Now your infinite Consciousness comes to know its existence through the form and says 'I exist!'

As your Consciousness comes to know its existence only through the form,

It accepts the form as itself unknowingly... though it is prior to form!

Your Consciousness is the source of entire manifestations and all forms... including your form... just now!

This you are yet to know!

You never remain Conscious of yourself to know this!

What is this 'I am ness'... Consciousness?

How to know it?

Only by closing your eyes...

Just now...!

You know the peace within just now...!

Just abide in this stillness constantly to know that your 'I am ness' Consciousness contains the seed of entire manifestations perceived here in space!

This world, every form perceived in space, cosmos, universe etc., are spontaneously, happening out of your 'I am ness' Consciousness just now!

Everything begins in your 'I am ness'!

Everything ends up in 'I am ness'!

But for your 'I am ness' Consciousness nothing appears, happens here!

There are never any persons here!

All forms are Conscious forms!

Entire functioning of the total manifestation is spontaneously happening in your 'I am ness' Consciousness by Consciousness itself!

When cosmos, world and all forms happen spontaneously in your 'I am ness' just now... in your Consciousness...

Who is the Observer of all that happen in your Consciousness?

You are That!

You are the Supreme Reality just now!

Only in your Consciousness, everything happens including your form and other forms, cosmos, world etc...

Your Consciousness happens only for a shorter duration say from waking state till sleep happens!

You take all that happen within Conscious field as real...as you are yet to know what this Consciousness is!

You, the Observer prevail forever!

You neither born nor die...!

Only in your Consciousness forms appear and disappear!

Whatever perceived in Conscious field as forms are not real, they are just a dream only!

You, the Observer are prior to dream!

Nothing never happens to you!

You alone prevail here as the Observer!

When everything that appears in Conscious field is nothing but a dream...

To whom those dream forms belong to?

Tell me!

You never know you are inside the dream and asking this as you take this form to be more real...not knowing that you are The Observer prior to form already!

You are yet to wake up from the dream called form, world etc.,

When you alone prevail here with no beginning and no ending and whatever Perceived in space are nothing but a dream...

Tell me!

To whom the dream form inside a dream belongs to?

Is the dream form real?

When it is real... why should it disappear upon waking?

Better wake up Consciously... from the dream called world and...

Know that you are The Ultimate!

You are already the Non Dual...!

Yet to explore it...!

...gm...

Q: Beloved GM, What is Personality?

GM:

Know! You are already the Supreme...!

You are formless, nameless and attributeless...!

You are Never born...Ever present...The Only Reality...!

You are already beyond Consciousness...you do not depend on Consciousness...! Rather it is Consciousness which depends on you...

You are always in your Original state only...!

Whether you know yourself or not......

Nothing has never happened to you...!

It is your 'I am' Consciousness asking this question...

Why are you bothered about the personality?

It is not you...!

Because you take yourself to be a form with a fixed name and functioning with many more identities imposed on you.

Your Consciousness unknowingly identifies itself as a form...!

By identifying yourself as 'I am' Consciousness you are relieved from the personality...!

Then it is possible for your Consciousness to know its Supreme Nature.

As long as your Consciousness identifies itself as a form... born on such and such a time...

It is impossible to know your Original Ultimate Truth.

Your Consciousness knows itself through the form as 'I am'... but it is not the form.

It uses the form but it is more than the form.

Consciousness is Universal...!

It pervades everywhere...!

Unknowingly it is limiting itself as a tiny form with a finite shape and volume and has a constant fear of losing the form... though it is beyond form!

Once you are in touch with a Realized, your 'I am' Consciousness starts waking up from the so called personality dream...!

Of course, personality is a sheer dream by Consciousness...!

Can any dream be True?

So also your personality...

Your Consciousness which is trapped by the personality dream should wake up by knowing that 'I am' is Consciousness only... at present... and not the imposed labels saying that I am this... and that...!

Then it is possible for the Consciousness to wake up from the dream...or else it is deceived by the so called birth and death which do not exist.

Only forms appear and disappear in Consciousness... taking the form to be a person is the greatest mistake.

When you identify yourself as a form, you are ignoring the indwelling Conscious principle within the form.

Can there be a form if you are not Conscious?

Can there be a world or cosmos if you are not Conscious?

Even your so called memory exists only in your Consciousness...

It is a great wonder how you are continuously deceived by these concepts that you are born...and you are only the form and so on...not knowing... the Conscious principle by which you see and know the world... without which there can be neither the world nor the manifestations.

Consciousness not knowing itself is personality...!

Once it knows that it is Consciousness only at present...then it can easily transcend itself too and remain free from its dream!

Know! As long as you consider yourself to be born and identifying yourself as a form... ignoring the Consciousness within...your dream continues and you cannot remain peaceful... though you are the Supreme...!

Why not you dare to understand all that have been expounded here and remain Conscious and get to know your Supreme Truth?

Why do you stoop down to the personality level?

Where is the need for you?

You are an emperor...now begging in the streets due to personality as you want to upgrade your personality to a maximum famous figure so that the world should never forget you...!

I ask you, "Where does your world exist?"

"Can there be a world... if you are not Conscious?'

"Can there be anything at all when you are no more Conscious?"

"Why not you pay attention on your 'I am' Consciousness?"

Then you will never ask this type of question which is dragging you down again to a dream state!

When are you going to wake up?

As you are still holding onto personality, where is the personality for That which is never born?

Are you That which is never born? Or

Were you born?

Which is True?

Which is born?

Find out by yourself......!

Right from the beginning you only Observe...!

Rest happens spontaneously...!

...gm...

3. THE OBSERVER PREVAILS PRIOR TO CONSCIOUSNESS

Q: Beloved GM, what is the Source of Consciousness?

GM:

First know!

You are Conscious of yourself at present.

In your 'I am ness' Consciousness only this question happens!

But you never know that you are Conscious only Just Now...

You are continuously trapped by all that perceived in space as real.

Your 'I am ness' Consciousness only manifests entire cosmos, universe, world and all forms that happen in space.

This... your Consciousness is yet to know!

To know this you need to close your eyes and abide within... constantly in stillness... beyond movement!

You see the light within and come to know that Light is Consciousness!

In the light of Consciousness, entire manifestation is reflected in space as objects.

Now your Consciousness knows all that perceived are not real!

Your Consciousness arises out of Awareness, manifests entire cosmos, world, universe and all forms including your form...within space.

In your 'I am ness' only everything appears, happens and disappears too...

In deep sleep you do not know your presence.

Only upon the arrival of Consciousness as 'I am ness' you know your presence which you call as waking state...

The world appears in your Consciousness only for a shorter duration say till sleep happens!

When Consciousness disappears in sleep, the world also disappears.

Your 'I am ness' is known only for a shorter duration... throughout the waking state...not in sleep.

Know! There is one state which Prevails prior to the arrival of Consciousness...as well even after the disappearance of Consciousness!

That which Prevails forever is Awareness...

The Source of your Consciousness... Just Now...!

Awareness Prevails prior to waking, dream and sleep states.

Awareness, the Observer Prevail prior to Consciousness!

Your Consciousness first accepts itself as a person unknowingly as a tiny form!

After seeing a Realized it knows its beyondness by closing eyes, stabilizing in stillness constantly, transcends itself and merges totally in its Source of Awareness and knows its Eternity beyond Birth and Death!

Your 'I am ness' initially accepts itself as a person!

Then it knows that it is Consciousness only and not the form!

Further at the Conscious level it transcends itself and knows the deathlessness...Only after merging totally in its Source of Awareness!

Awareness - The Source- Is Ever Here!

You are That!

In Awareness, your Consciousness happens!

In your Consciousness the world happens!

But you are neither the Consciousness nor the form within space.

You are always the Observer...prior to Consciousness!

The Source of Consciousness which your Consciousness is yet to know!

Simply Observe silently...!
Through Observation you remain free from the play...!

...gm...

Q: *Beloved GM, What do you Mean by Exactly... "Nothing Never Happens Here!" Could you please say something about it?*

GM:

Now your Consciousness is asking clarification for this statement that Nothing Never Happens...

As it is yet to wake up totally to know this!

Now you know that you exist only due to Consciousness within!

Now, you know that you exist!

Is it not?

But you do not know what you are exactly!

Still your 'I am ness' Consciousness identifies itself as a form only with certain labels and functions with such identities only... taking all happenings to be more real here!

Your Consciousness identifies itself as a tiny form not knowing its infinity Just Now!

It is your Consciousness which manifests the entire world but never knows this Truth!

It is your Consciousness that functions through the entire manifestations...!

This also your Consciousness never knows!

It is your Consciousness that drops all forms!

This also your Consciousness never knows!

Why?

Because your Consciousness is yet to know itself!

Still, it is trapped by the form level identity strongly and unwilling to know that it is only Consciousness within and not the form that appear!

Through form level identity... it goes on extending its dream as a personality...!

There is no remedy at this dream level personality.

It is strongly conditioning itself as a person unknowingly... and accepts all imposed knowledge as real!

It accepts all happenings within space to be real...as it is yet to wake up from the dream by personality!

It never knows that whatever appears as objects... Just Now in space are nothing but a reflection of light within!

Consciousness knows that it is Consciousness only by going deeper inwardly...and knowing the stillness within!

Through stillness it knows the light within!

Once light is known...it knows that the entire manifestation is only a reflection of light within space!

It knows that the elements are created out of light spontaneously!

Created elements interact spontaneously at a greater speed in no time with innumerable permutations of combinations and objects appear...only by the elemental interaction!

But for the light neither the elements nor any objects in space here!

Light is the base for the entire manifestation...!

Consciousness abides in stillness consistently and transcends itself and knows its Eternity beyond duality!

It knows that it is never born but ever present!

Where is the death for the one that which is never born?

It knows that what is born is only a sheer dream by the spontaneous elemental interactions!

Having known all that perceived in space are only a dream by the spontaneous elemental display, will it fall a prey to such dreams?

Once Consciousness wakes up totally... it is relieved from the duality called Birth and Death!

Consciousness in ignorance accepts the dream as real...!

Once Consciousness wakes up totally...

It knows its beyondness prior to dream!

Consciousness after waking up totally knows its Wholeness!

Now it declares that Nothing Never Happens!

All that were perceived were only an Unreal dream!

There is not even an iota of Truth in all that perceived in space!

When?

Only upon waking up Consciously...Totally... Not until then...!

You are already the Supreme! The Non Dual!

Nothing never happens to you!

Even now!

Still, you are caught by every happening in space as more real!

Why?

Your Consciousness is yet to wake up totally now from the present dream itself!

Your Consciousness can wake up only by listening to a Realized who has transcended the duality...!

Only the awakened one... beyond the duality dream can guide you and wake up your Consciousness which is still struggling by accepting all events as real including the birth of the form...!

Why I go on emphasize that your Consciousness has to wake up from the present dream?

Because... I am the Source itself!

I know what this 'Consciousness is'...!

I, the Absolute Prevail prior to Consciousness!

Only I can guide your Consciousness to wake up now from the dream called Birth and Death and make you aware of what you are exactly now...that you are the Ever present Ultimate already and nothing never happened to you...as you are never born!

What is born is not you... but an unreal dream!

At least now, will you listen deeply and wake up... to know that Nothing Never Happens?

Present itself is moving faster...!
You cannot hold anything to be more Real here...!

...gm...

Q: Beloved GM, What exists?

GM:

Know first! That Whatever Appears to Exist is not Real...!

Where do they all exist?

In your 'I am' Consciousness only...!

Is it not?

Entire manifestations and the whole beauty of it is a Miracle only...!

The Whole existence is just a miracle only...happening in your Consciousness...

Just Now...!

You see flowers, Rivers, Mountains, whole cosmos, Birds and all appearances and you are enticed by the beauty of the entire manifestations...!

Entire bundle of perceived manifestation is nothing but a miracle by 'I am' Consciousness...!

Not knowing where they happen and how they happen... Whether all are real or not...you simply see and say you are lost in its Beauty...!

Do you ever know that whatever you perceive is by your Consciousness Only?

You are inviting the creator unnecessarily not knowing that the whole creation is by your 'I am' Consciousness only... Just Now!

At the personality level, you are yet to know what Consciousness is...!

So you say, 'All is by the Creator'!

Can there be any creations without the creator?

Can there be any world without your Consciousness?

Your Consciousness is the creator...creating the world...Just Now in your Conscious field.

There are no persons.

When all that exist is True, then why do they disappear?

Your world exists when 'I am' Consciousness happens and ends up...when 'I am' Consciousness is no more.

Existence of the World, Cosmos, Universe depend on your 'I am' Consciousness.

Where do they all exist now?

In your 'I am' Consciousness only...!

How do you know that you exist?

Through 'I am' Consciousness only...!

Can you know if the form is not available?

This form is necessary to know the 'I am' Consciousness within...!

'I am' Consciousness within is a biochemical with sensors...!

It contains the seed of the entire manifestations within.

Through the form this 'I am' Consciousness reflects itself as cosmos, universe etc., in space...!

Whatever perceived in space is only a reflection of light...!

Not Real...!

They appear to exist but not so...exactly like seeing a film on the screen where you see...a hero chasing someone... singing and dancing with a heroine...

You see only a reflected image in the screen but it appears so real...!

Similarly, even now whatever you perceive in space is only the reflection of 'I am' Consciousness within...not real...!

Whatever that happens within Conscious field is nothing but an Entertainment only...!

No reality in it...

Consciousness is entertaining itself...as there are no persons here...!

This you will know only when you see the light within... which is Ever Here... but you are yet to see...!

You are bothered only about that which exists for a while…!

Have you known the Observer of all that appear to exist?

Is not the Observer prior to existence?

Observer Prevails Forever… Unbothered… whether something exists… or not…!

You, the Observer are already beyond waking, sleep and dream states…!

You Prevail Forever… whether Consciousness happens or not…!

See how you were caught by the show by the 'I am' Consciousness now!

Primary miracle is the spontaneous happening of your 'I am' Consciousness…!

Secondary Miracle is the spontaneous happening of the entire manifestations such as world, Cosmos, Universe in your 'I am' Consciousness simultaneously…!

Third miracle is Consciousness being deceived by its own reflected images as real… as it does not know itself…!

Throughout the waking state these miracles by 'I am' Consciousness go on… due to the play of the five elements…

Final miracle is… the world disappearing with the disappearance of 'I am' Consciousness…!

This miracle is endless and the deception too endless...till Consciousness knows its Supreme Source...!

Consciousness not knowing itself is the greatest miracle...!

Once your Consciousness is Awakened, then you are free from this dreamy Existence and know your Supreme Truth beyond the manifested Existence.

Till then you are caught by this dreamy world and its show as more real... Unknowingly...!

When are you going to wake up from this Non existing dreamy world which appears to exist?

Better start waking up at least now...!

By accepting the personality as your identity
You feel yourself separate from the others...!

Q: Dear GM, What is subject and object here? Am I the subject or the object?

What am I exactly?

GM:

Your 'I am ness' Consciousness is your subject!

Only in your 'I am ness' everything appears now!

But for your 'I am ness' there is neither the manifestations nor any objects in space!

Consciousness accepts itself as a tiny form here in space!

By accepting itself as a form... it remains bothered about all the objects in space!

Your Consciousness never knows that all objects are from itself... just now!

Your Consciousness is trapped at the personality level...!

So it accepts itself as a tiny form within space!

Not only your form but all forms within space,

Where do they all appear?

Is it not in your 'I am ness' Consciousness just now?

Unknowingly your Consciousness first accepts itself as a tiny form (an object) with a fixed shape and mass!

This identification as an object is at the form level identity only!

Once your Consciousness is Conscious of itself... it starts knowing that it is the subject from which all objects appear!

Object - at the form level identity!

Subject - at the Conscious level!

This object and subject identifications are only within space in your Consciousness!

You, the Observer are prior to Consciousness just now!

You are neither the subject!

Nor the object in space!

You, the Absolute prevail prior to Consciousness!

You, the Absolute are prior to dream already!

Subject and objects are only a dream in space and none of them real!

Subject and object... all such divisions are only in duality!

You, the Observer are non dual!

Subject and object appear to disappear...!

You, the Absolute are beyond all appearances!

You are ever present here!

Subject and object have a beginning and an ending too!

You, the Absolute have no beginning and no ending...!

Subject and object are incomplete by themselves as they appear and disappear!

You, the Absolute are Total, Complete and Perfect!

Know!

Your Consciousness (subject) remains incomplete at the form (object) level identity!

Once your Consciousness (subject) is Conscious of itself and knows the stillness within, it starts waking up from the manifested (object) dream and transcends itself!

By transcending itself into its Source of Awareness... it knows its eternity and declares birth and death are only a dream...and not real!

Why don't you know at least now that...

You are The Absolute...!

The Ultimate...!

The Supreme...!

Beyond space...!

Beyond all divisions...as subject and object...?

Know this Truth......provided you wake up from the dream Consciously...

Just now!

Will you?

Be an ordinary Being...!

Live Effortlessly...!

Q: Beloved GM, if I am Consciousness, why am I identified with mind and body?

GM:

You are Conscious already.!

Or else how can you ask this question?

It is your Consciousness asking this question as it is not aware of itself.

First you become Conscious of yourself.

In your Consciousness only, body and thoughts happen.

If you are not Conscious... where is the body and thought?

Your Consciousness happens first, in your Consciousness only body and thoughts appear. Is it not?

Instead of giving preference to Consciousness, you give preference to body and thought.

Form is needed for the Consciousness to know its presence as 'I am ness'.

Though Consciousness is everywhere, it knows its presence as 'I am ness' only through a physical matrix called form!

Similarly, thoughts also help you.

Consciousness is the Master!

Form and thoughts are your servants.

Consciousness means you know that you exist without words.

Your direct knowing about your existence.

Once you go within, you will gradually know the peacefulness within.

Then your Consciousness guides you.

Remain Conscious and make use of the form and thought like a king using all paraphernalia for his empire.

Live like an emperor, not less than that. But identify your Self only as Consciousness...!

See clearly, everything as a play happening in your Consciousness by Consciousness itself.

You feel relieved as an Observer.

You are in Supreme state always but could not realize it due to Conscious play.

So, knowledge of Consciousness is most important.

In deep sleep you remain peaceful.

After the arrival of Consciousness, you miss peacefulness though it is here now.

So Consciousness has to know itself...!

Entire movement within space is a play by Consciousness.

I know peacefulness which is endless and infinite as I am aware of what this Consciousness is...!

There is not even an iota of Truth in the field of Consciousness.

So why bother about any happening which is not True?

Your inner Richness is ever here...!

It is prior to dream...!

Just now...!

...gm...

4. YOU, THE OBSERVER NEVER DO ANYTHING

Q: Beloved GM, Mind to No - Mind... this journey is possible?

GM:

Thought to no thought...

You cannot travel from thought to no thought!

Are you a thought?

Are you not Conscious of yourself now?

Don't you perceive thoughts in your Consciousness just now?

Can thoughts happen if you are not Conscious of yourself?

Your question indicates that you are yet to know that you are Conscious only at present!

Your Consciousness unknowingly identifies a thought as itself...

Hence asking... thought to no thought journey is possible?

Your Consciousness is ever here...!

You are already Consciousness only just now!

Unnecessarily your Consciousness identifies itself as a thought not knowing it is Consciousness only just now!

How to know that you are Conscious only now?

Just close your eyes!

Know the peace, stillness within!

This is the beginning of your Consciousness!

Know the immense beauty of your Consciousness!

Your Consciousness is the source of entire manifestation within space!

Without your Consciousness...neither the cosmos nor the universe nor any living being here!

Entire manifestation depends on your 'I am ness' Consciousness just now!

Once you abide in stillness within... you know that your Consciousness is the base for everything that appears in space!

Know you are an emperor already...!

Know your richness inwardly!

Without knowing your inner richness you fall a prey to a single thought and accept that you are just a thought and want to travel from thought to no - thought...

Impossible!

You are right now Consciousness only!

No need to travel to know this!

Just closing eyes is enough now!

Know the stillness within right now!

Know you are Conscious of yourself without words!

Thoughts are just words!

You are prior to words...!

To know your wordless state... stillness... which is a non movement...

What journey... or movement is needed?

Tell me!

Movements are needed only to use words...

No movement is needed to know your Consciousness within which is prior to words!

Only from this stillness everything appears and moves!

Know this!

Stillness is unmoving...Within right now...

It is prior to all movements in space!

No movement is required to know yourself just now!

Be still...!

And know...no journey is needed to be yourself...!

You are right now Consciousness only...!

No need to travel to know this...!

...gm...

Q: 'Just Be!' - Dear GM, Can you explain on this?

GM:

Just be means simply Observe...without involvement...

As your Consciousness identifies all as Real... it goes on identifying and manipulating endlessly without rest.

You are already the Observer only... beyond Consciousness!

But you never know your Beyondness!

You are caught up by all the play happenings within space... Unknowingly and remain restless!

You, the Observer, never do anything...!

You only Observe all that happen within Conscious field as the world, Cosmos as manifestations silently!

Only in your Observation the world, cosmos happen...! Just Now...!

Is it not?

But for your Consciousness there is neither the world nor any cosmos or anything.

Know! It is your Consciousness which creates everything... just now within space and starts functioning through the entire manifestations.

Your Consciousness and the world are not separate!

All activities like breathing, heartbeat, metabolic activities are spontaneously going on without any effort by you!

Do you make any effort for the same?

Each and every activity is spontaneous by your Consciousness!

You never do anything...

All actions are by Consciousness itself!

You may say 'I am eating......Walking......doing all actions!'

My question is can there be any action at all... if you are not Conscious?

All actions are by your 'I am ness' Consciousness Only...!

But you say, "I am doing it"... as you still identify yourself as a limited form with a fixed shape.

Can your form function without Consciousness?

Know the lively principle... 'I am ness' Consciousness which does all the work spontaneously!

So you never do anything!

All by Consciousness only!

When all actions are by Consciousness...then who is the Observer of all those actions?

You are the Observer...

Observing silently all that happen within Space Just Now!

You the Observer never do anything!

The Observer is Unchanging, Unmoving...and Ever present...!

You are That!

You never knew that you are already the Observer......

Beyond... Consciousness and its expressions as the world, cosmos etc.,

Only in your Consciousness everything appears to happen and disappears.

But you the Observer Prevail here forever beyond dualities...!

You the Observer never do anything!

You only Observe!

Just Now!

Just be – means simply Observe through stillness......as this stillness is connected to the Source to know your immense potential beyond all divisions...

Just be...

Does not mean that you should not do any work...

It means just Observe...all that happen within Conscious field through stillness!

Know!

It is Consciousness that carries out all the work necessary for the survival of the form as it needs the form to know itself!

Don't interfere with the Conscious play and simply Observe!

You simply Observe... Just Now!

Breathing and all actions through the form are by Consciousness itself... Just Now!

Do you accept at least now that you never do anything and only Observe?

You will accept it provided you stay beyond words and abide in stillness...!

Simply Observe silently...!
Through Observation you
Remain free from the play...!

...gm...

Q: *Beloved GM, How to control thoughts?*

GM:

Thoughts are not you!

They are just movements within space.

Thoughts do not have a dwelling place.

They simply move...

When thoughts are not you, why do you bother?

You are Conscious at present!

You know that 'you exist' now...

Just stay here.

In your 'I am ness' Consciousness, thoughts happen.

Thoughts are only for utility.

Just use them when needed.

Simply Observe silently!

When you attend every thought, you are imparting more energy to it.

Then thought becomes your Master and starts dictating you!

You become a slave to a single thought by imparting more and more energy by focusing attention on it...

You become very tired as your energy is drained off by a single thought which is not you!

Thoughts do not have life at all!

Your Consciousness is more alive!

Your Consciousness is the Source of energy!

When you simply Observe a thought… without involvement… you don't spend energy on it.

So you are not affected by that thought.

When you involve so much with a single thought…you impart more energy and become too tired as more energy is spent on a single thought.

You never know what you are exactly!

You give importance to thoughts as you take all thoughts to be Real.

Why not you focus attention on your 'I am ness' Consciousness within, instead of focusing attention on a non existing thought?

Once you know that you are Conscious only at present…this moment… your Conscious presence is more than enough!

You remain calm, cool and Observe silently all that happen around you!

Once you close your eyes and know the stillness within…you will not be disturbed by any thought that happens around you.

You are asking, How to control thoughts?

Can you control something which is not you?

For example, a huge procession is going... on the road...

Will you try to control that procession and its movement?

Every happening is spontaneous and none of the happenings are you!

Thought also just happens!

Do not involve with its movements!

Simply Observe!

Do not identify them...

When you do not involve... you are already free from thoughts!

By involving much...you impart more energy and get caught by thoughts.

Know!

You cannot control any happening within space!

Can you control your breathing?

Heart beat? Blood circulation?

Why?

Because they all happen spontaneously...Just Now...without your involvement!

Your job is only to Observe silently without words!

Observe silently through stillness and know that thoughts do not exist at all...!

Only your Consciousness 'I am ness' exists now!

Once you know your unending peace and endless joy within, you will not be perturbed by the moving thoughts!

You will use them when essential, as you are the Master now!

Thoughts become your assistant... they help you to live comfortably within space.

Now you, the Master, use thoughts conveniently!

Now there is no need to control thoughts!

In your 'I am ness' Consciousness only... they happen for a shorter duration.

You just make use of them!

You remain a Master Forever!

Can you?

Real freedom is to be with yourself...!

...gm...

Q: *Beloved GM, How to make my life Outwardly Rich and also Inwardly Rich?*

Is *there any secret? Kindly explain!*

GM:

What do you mean by Richness?

Is it to possess something greater than the other?

Here in space no one is rich...!

No one is poor!

Richness...with reference to what?

Is there any threshold limit to assess it?

I say... there are never any persons here!

All forms are existing now... only in your 'I am ness' Consciousness...Just Now!

But for your 'I am ness' Consciousness nothing is here in space!

This question is at the personality level...!

Are you a person?

Are you not Conscious of yourself now?

How do you know that you exist?

Can this question be asked if you are no more Conscious of yourself?

Why don't you focus attention on yourself Just Now?

Your 'I am ness' Consciousness contains all...!

Without your 'I am ness' Consciousness ...

Neither manifestations nor any forms here in space including your form Just Now!

You never know your immense Richness inwardly!

I mean Richness which is fullness and Completeness!

Inwardly you are already Rich...Total and Complete!

You are yet to know your Inner Richness!

By not knowing your Inner Richness... your Consciousness simply accepts itself as a tiny form with fixed labels and starts moving here and there... in search of Outer Richness!

There is nothing called Richness outside here!

All your Richness are only a dream here!

What is a dream display?

Is any of the display in dream...Real?

Money is a useful convention for a convenient livelihood.

Know you are more than that!

First know your Consciousness contains all...!(Entire universe, cosmos, the world, all living beings in space and space itself!)

Where do all that perceived here exist?

In space only!

But for space neither any object nor any manifestations here!

Where does space exist?

Is it not in your 'I am ness' Consciousness Just Now?

Your Consciousness is within...Just Now!

You know this through stillness...Just Now!

Your Consciousness is the base for the entire objects Observed in space!

You are an Emperor inwardly...Just Now!

Without your Consciousness nothing can appear in space including space itself!

Your Consciousness is prior to space!

It contains the seeds of the entire manifestation within Just Now which you are yet to explore...!

Not knowing that you are an Emperor already inwardly... you are moving here and there inside a dream... in search of Richness!

There is nothing here in space other than the reflections of the light within...!

None of the perceived is Real...like a dream display...!

Your Consciousness unknowingly moves here and there to remain rich outwardly!

Outwardly in space there is nothing called Richness here!

All are constantly changing... none of them are permanent and Real...!

That is why outwardly your Consciousness is under great stress and remains fearful of losing its possessions.

When everything is changing at a greater speed in no time Just Now... and none of them are Real......

Can your Consciousness remain richest constantly here...?

When all that perceived are constantly moving and changing... what can your Consciousness hold to be Real here?

That is why your Consciousness gets frustrated frequently by outer happenings!

Your Consciousness tries to hold the dream happenings as more real...!

Why?

Because it is yet to know its inner Richness which is unchanging and unmoving... and Ever present within right now!

Everything begins in your 'I am ness' Consciousness and ends up in your 'I am ness' Consciousness!

What more you need than your 'I am ness' Consciousness now?

Once your Consciousness starts knowing that it is Consciousness only within...It abides in stillness constantly... and knows its Supreme Richness beyond dualities!

Know...!

What you call as outer Richness... is only a dream... not Real...!

Your inner Richness is Ever Here!

It is prior to dream! Just Now!

Your Source contains everything...!

Till you know your Inner Richness you move in search of dream objects as outer Richness...!

Once you know what 'You are exactly...'!

Then you know what is... Real Richness......

which has no beginning and no ending...!

You contain it already now...!

Just close your eyes and explore your Supreme Richness which Prevails here forever in immense beauty beyond divisions...!

By remaining Conscious of yourself... you remain rich inwardly!

When you are no more Conscious of yourself... you miss your Richness!

That is why going on accumulating things endlessly not knowing they are just dream objects only!

Once your Consciousness wakes up... it knows its unchanging Richness forever...!

Till then it is trapped by its own dream at the personality level... by accepting all dream events as Real!

Now tell me!

Is it not more essential to wake up and know what you are exactly?

That you are the Absolute...

Non Dual......

Ever present Here...Infinite...and Endless...

The Ultimate already Just Now!

Better wake up and know now!

Will you?

All Meditation techniques are only

To know the stillness within Just Now...!

Q: *Beloved GM, "Prior to knowledge" – Could you please explain more on this?*

GM:

You are already prior to knowledge!

What is knowledge?

Some detail about any object, any happenings.

First of all, how do you know anything?

What is the principle without which there is neither yourself nor any manifestations?

What is the principle without which you can never know yourself?

How do you know that you exist?

Is it not due to your 'I am ness' Consciousness?

The primary knowledge is...the knowing that you exist!

In your existence only all else appear to happen and disappear too.

In deep sleep you don't know that you exist!

You come to know your existence only upon the arrival of 'I am ness' in your waking state.

This 'I am ness' is your direct knowing.

You need not ask anyone whether you exist.

You, yourself know it on your own.

It is self-evident!

This 'I am ness' knowing is spontaneous and independent!

In this 'I am ness'...you know the peace within.

You remain still.

This is prior to words.

Any knowledge about any object including your form is an additional knowledge only.

Any knowledge is dependent...!

Knowledge depends on some objects.

Your 'I am ness' is prior to all knowledge which depend on materials.

'I am ness' is your direct knowing.

Only in your 'I am ness' Consciousness every knowledge is received including the knowledge about your form that you are so and so...and all forms around you!

Tell me, are you the imposed knowledge?

Are not all the imposed knowledge exist only in your 'I am ness' Consciousness Just Now?

Can there be any knowledge when you are not Conscious?

In deep sleep you don't know that you exist!

Spontaneously you know that 'you exist'.

This 'I am ness' is your primary knowledge!

Rest of the knowledge are imposed on you!

They are not you!

Are you an object?

Are you not the subject without which there is neither the world nor any object?

Know your greatness!

Know your immense beauty!

Know your Supreme Richness!

Then you will not fall a prey to any knowledge which are not you!

In deep sleep you don't know that you exist!

But now you know that you exist.

This knowing your existence is wakefulness.

Just Now you know that you exist...without words.

This knowing, wakefulness is prior to all imposed knowledge!

Knowing your presence without words is wakefulness!

This stillness is wakefulness!

Are you not wakeful now?

Now, you are wakeful, Conscious of yourself!

In this 'I am ness' Consciousness... only every knowledge is received.

Now tell me, are you not prior to knowledge Just Now?

Know you are an Emperor Already...!

Know your Richness inwardly Right Now...!

...gm...

5. WISDOM IS YOUR DIRECT KNOWING

Q:Beloved GM, how to be Conscious of ourselves? I know that 'I am' Conscious. I can feel things, I can eat, sleep, work, and think. Is this what you mean by being Conscious of yourself?

GM:

Conscious means knowing your presence here...

Just close your eyes.

You know the peace within.

Now, you know that you exist without words.

Your knowing is direct about your presence.

It is self evident.

You need not ask anyone whether you exist.

This peace is the beginning of Consciousness.

Once you abide in this stillness...

You are beyond Time and Words.

Your Consciousness simply sees and responds.

Consciousness functions out of peacefulness...

Once you are peaceful and joyful inwardly...it shows you are Conscious of yourself.

You remain stabilized and more clear of what you do or say.

You will see clarity in your actions and words.

You will be brighter and you don't require any guidance from outside.

Your Consciousness guides you.

Once you are Conscious, you value neither the past nor the future!

Your Consciousness itself is enough for you.

You will not long for anything and you will make use of whatever is available to you and start enjoying your presence wherever you are and whatever you do.

Your Consciousness contains all.

Once you are Conscious of yourself ...You are the Master!

In your Consciousness, only thoughts appear and disappear...

You simply Observe thoughts and use them if needed or else you ignore them.

You remain calm and cool as you know that nothing can be done and the total functioning of the entire manifestation in your Consciousness are Spontaneous!

You know that you are Consciousness only and more than the form...

You know that there are never any persons but all by Consciousness itself...

By remaining Conscious of yourself, Your Consciousness starts waking up from the dream called the past or the future and abides in the present moment silently...

By Observing the present moment constantly through stillness, it gets to know that whatever that is perceived is neither constant nor Real.

The more it Observes silently, it is merging in its Source of Awareness.

It transcends itself and knows its Truth beyond Birth and Death...

It knows its Supreme Richness!

Now, tell me... is it not essential to be Conscious of yourself?

When there are no persons...!

All forms are by Consciousness itself...!

What is born?

What can die?

...gm...

Q: *Beloved GM, What is True Wisdom?*

GM:

Wisdom is prior to all knowledge!

Wisdom is your direct knowing.

You know that you exist now!

This knowing your existence as 'I am' ...without words is wisdom.

Your existence is self evident.

Knowledge is dependent.

To know something other than you... you need knowledge...

To know yourself, your presence, you don't require any external knowledge!

Your knowing is direct and independent of outer knowledge...!

Only in your wisdom, in your 'I am ness'... Consciousness... The knowledge about every object is received...

Knowledge depends on objects other than you!

Your knowing... wisdom...is your own subject...!

Knowledge is limited...!

Knowing... is Unlimited...!

Knowledge is finite...!

Knowing is infinite...!

Knowledge is only a theory...indirect...!

Knowing is practical...direct...!

Knowledge is not you!

Knowing is by yourself...!

But for your Consciousness, you cannot know anything here including your existence.

First you know that 'you exist'!

This is wisdom!

Only in your 'I am ness' Consciousness everything appears, happens and disappears too...

Your 'I am ness' Consciousness is the Source of the entire manifestation!

Knowing this...is wisdom!

To accept that you are the form with certain labels attached to it is...only a knowledge...It is not wisdom!

Through knowledge your Consciousness is conditioning itself......

Through wisdom your Consciousness is Conscious of itself and remains free from all conditionings...

Your Question is... What is True Wisdom?

Wisdom is knowing oneself as Consciousness at present and remaining free from the gathered knowledge.

Wisdom is to remain unburdened, free from all knowledge gathered...

Wisdom is to know that everything within space is by Consciousness itself and nothing is alien to itself.

Wisdom is to know that every action is spontaneous here ... and there are never any persons!

Wisdom is to know all that happen in space is by Consciousness itself and there is nothing apart from it!

Do you know that you are only the Wisdom prior to knowledge and not the knowledge......at least now?

Fearlessness is not a movement outside...!

But knowing the Unmoving Centre Within and

Observing silently all that happen in space...!

...gm...

Q: Beloved GM, In full Awareness...only nothingness is there. How can I know that awakened state?

GM:

There is nothing called full Awareness as it cannot be partial.

Know that Awareness is always fullness only as it is Complete by itself, totally independent.

How do you say only nothingness is there?

What do you mean by nothingness?

You mean nothingness with respect to the absence of objects?

For example, when a room is full of furniture, you say room is full.

When all furniture is removed, you say the room is empty.

You mean this as nothing?

But do you know that the room is full of space only... previously occupied by objects...now free from objects...?

But space is there without which object cannot happen.

In your Consciousness only space happens... simultaneously entire manifestations appear in space.

All objects are objectified in space and move in space.

This movement is termed as time.

So, space and time happen in your Consciousness.

At once you are caught by the objects in space and their movements as time...!

But you the Absolute are beyond space and beyond time.

Once Consciousness happens, you are caught by the space and all the play happenings in space and time.

When you close your eyes, you see nothing inside.

It is not nothingness.

It is full of potential.

It contains the seed of the entire manifestation within.

Out of this nothingness only, entire cosmos, world and all innumerable forms happen.

If you know this, can you call this as nothingness?

Only those who do not know the seed of Consciousness call it as nothingness.

No! It is not nothingness...!

It is full of potential...it contains the entire manifestation in nascent stage.

With what Identity you are asking this question?

You are asking, how can I know the awakened state?

At the Conscious level you can only remain Conscious......
rest happens.

In sleep, dreams appear and you perceive unknowingly all as
real...is it not?

Once you wake up, you know that all were dreams only,
unreal.

Similarly, in this Conscious field innumerable forms are
created in your Consciousness and all function in your
Consciousness and you take everything to be real...Not
knowing that this waking state itself is a dream.

How will you know your awakened state as long as you take
the dreams to be real?

Awakening is Here, Now...!

Not somewhere...far.

Your Consciousness awakens once it subsides in Awareness
totally.

Then your Consciousness is no more there.

It becomes Awareness only.

Now, tell me,

Who is here to know the awakened state?

After waking up neither Consciousness nor forms –

Only unmoving...... Ever present Awareness!

Know the entire play of movements by

Simply remaining in Unmoving stillness!

...gm...

Q: Beloved GM, What is Self Realization?

GM:

Self means your Consciousness which knows its presence through the form as 'I am ness'.

Your Consciousness has to know what it is as it is trapped by the personality identity by accepting itself as a tiny form unknowingly!

A Realized says:

'You are beyond Consciousness!

You are never born!

Whatever perceived is only a dream...not real!

Go within...and know!'

After listening to the Realized statement, your Consciousness starts remaining Conscious of itself and abides in stillness...

Once Consciousness goes inwardly deeply... it gets to know that the Source of the entire manifestation is within itself and nothing is separate from itself.

Consciousness accepts all that is perceived as real till it sees the light within!

Now, Consciousness knows that it is more than the form, the Source of all forms.

Further, Consciousness merges in its Source of Awareness and transcends itself totally and knows its Eternity beyond Birth and Death!

Consciousness is incomplete by accepting itself as a form... in the beginning...

After meeting a Realized, it knows its Unborn nature and remains complete.

This is Self Realization!

Consciousness which accepts the birth as real at the form level remains incomplete......

Hence Consciousness starts searching itself outside which is futile...as it is very much within!

Only by going inwardly it starts knowing its Source of Awareness and its Wholeness which is Non-Dual beyond Birth and Death.

First it accepts Birth and Death as Real... at the duality level...

After knowing its Source it knows its Wholeness beyond duality where there is neither the birth nor the death...

Only Eternity beyond all divisions!

Incomplete Consciousness through form identity... now remains complete after realizing its Unborn, Eternity!

Consciousness Knowing its Wholeness is Self Realization!

You are not the present moment...!

You are the Observer of the present moment...!

Q: Beloved GM, When you say Consciousness, you do not mean the mind? Do you? Mind happens within Consciousness, isn't it? And Consciousness isn't limited to the mind or body, correct? Consciousness contains everything isn't it?

GM:

Yes. Consciousness is Unlimited!

Infinite!

I don't use the word mind but thought.

Thoughts happen in your Consciousness.

Thoughts are not you. At present you are Consciousness.

Body, thoughts happen in your Consciousness.

They are not you.

Why bother about them…?

Focus your full attention on your Consciousness itself.

You know you are! (without words)

Just be! Stay there!

Stabilize there and settle there!

Rest happens!

Spontaneously your Consciousness

Wakes up totally.!

Never be in a hurry.!

Just Relax...!

Inwardly.!

...gm...

6. CONSCIOUSNESS NEEDS THE FORM TO KNOW ITSELF

Q: Beloved GM, Your Consciousness is now trapped by the personality with imposed labels! Can you explain on this?

GM:

What are you now?

Are you not Conscious of yourself now?

Do you ever know that you are Consciousness only at present?

Your Consciousness accepts itself as a form now.

Can the form function without Consciousness?

Can the world exist when you are not Conscious?

Can you know your form when you are not Conscious?

Where does your form exist?

Where does the world exist?

Have you ever pondered over on these lines?

In your 'I am ness' Consciousness only everything happens including your form Just Now!

This your Consciousness never knows.

Your Consciousness accepts itself as a tiny form with fixed labels... as itself... not knowing... its immense potential that there is neither the world nor any manifestations, here in space without your 'I am ness' Consciousness.

What are you now?

Are you the form?

You are more than the form!

But you accept yourself as a form!

You are none of the labels added on you!

You are beyond form!

Form cannot confine you!

You are beyond name!

Name cannot confine you!

You are beyond qualities!

Qualities cannot confine you!

You have no boundary!

Still you are confined at the personality level with fixed labels imposed on you unknowingly!

You are formless, nameless and attributeless...!

See how you are trapped by the personality at the form level... unknowingly and confine yourself... as certain labels.........

Not knowing... that the world and the entire manifestation happen out of your 'I am ness' Consciousness Just Now!

In your 'I am ness'…only the world happens now!

But for your 'I am ness' Consciousness… nothing is here!

Why don't you focus attention on yourself to know your greatness beyond all manifestations here…instead of attaching yourself with certain labels taking them to be Real?

Can you?

Nowhere to go!

But

Within.!

…gm…

Q: Beloved GM, Denying the form, Using the form – Which one is correct?

GM:

Where does the form exist now?

Is it not in your 'I am ness' Consciousness Just Now?

But for your Consciousness can the form exist?

First, you are Conscious of yourself as 'I am ness'...!

In your 'I am ness' Consciousness... not only your form...

But all forms exist Just Now!

You know the form only through your Consciousness!

When you are no more Conscious, form also cannot be known!

Your 'I am ness' Consciousness and form are not separate!

Know this first!

Consciousness is everywhere!

But it knows its presence only through the form as 'I am ness'...!

In your Consciousness only... form happens...Just Now!

Your Consciousness creates the form and functions through the form Just Now!

What is a form?

Is it not an accumulation of zillions and zillions of cells as a fixed shape and a mass?

Each and every cell is created by your Consciousness only Just Now!

Every metabolic activity is by your Consciousness only!

Consciousness Prevails prior to form!

Form happens Just Now in your Consciousness!

Your Consciousness is trapped by accepting itself as a tiny form not knowing its infinity beyond boundaries here in space!

Now your Consciousness is trapped by the form level identity... hence this question:

Your question: 'Denying the form or using the form – which one is correct'?

Unknowingly Your Consciousness asks this question as it does not know that it is using the form Just Now and asking this question!

See how it is trapped now!

You cannot deny the form as the form is necessary to know your existence as 'I am ness' now!

Only through the form, your Consciousness knows its existence as 'I am ness' now!

But your Consciousness wrongly accepts itself as a form... not knowing it is only Consciousness within... out of which all forms and entire manifestations happen spontaneously... Just Now!

Consciousness which knows its presence as 'I am ness' through the form should know that it is prior to form and only using the form now!

This form is an instrument like seeing a distant object through a telescope.

You see an object through a telescope.

Are you the telescope?

You are only using the telescope.

Similarly, here your Consciousness is only using the form!

You are using a musical instrument to play the music!

Are you the instrument?

Are you not using the instrument?

Just like that... this form is used by your Consciousness constantly throughout the waking state!

Consciousness needs this form to know itself!

Consciousness takes care of the form through constant intake of food at frequent intervals!

To the Consciousness, form is necessary to know itself!

To the form, food is essential to maintain itself!

You cannot deny food to the form!

By denying food... your form becomes weaker and without food... the form cannot be known through Consciousness!

Q: Denying the form, using the form – which one is correct?

By denying form what do you mean?

You mean denying food?

Your form cannot survive without food!

Food is enriched with Consciousness!

By denying food you are denying yourself which is Consciousness at present!

This form is woven out of Consciousness only Just Now!

Once you are Conscious of yourself by closing eyes and knowing the stillness within... then you remain calm and Conscious of whatever you do!

Once you are Conscious of yourself your Consciousness uses the form Consciously for worldly purposes.

Simultaneously your Consciousness starts knowing its immense potential within... prior to form arrival here!

By remaining Conscious of yourself through stillness... your Consciousness uses the form Consciously!

By not remaining Conscious of itself and accepting itself as a tiny form... it is not aware of its True nature within and asks this question... Unknowingly!

Now, tell Me.!

Is it not essential to be Conscious of yourself Just Now and know that you are prior to the form and only using the form to know your Supreme Richness?

Till Consciousness is known

You take everything

To be more Real...!

...gm...

Q: Dear GM, Realized one like you, how to mingle or manage with the world level activities?

GM:

Nothing is separate from Me!

I don't find any divisions here... as All are Myself only!

I remain quiet...!

I know what is happening around me in this world...!

I remain unconcerned about all such happenings.

I know what this Consciousness is............

Which plays here as manifestations within space!

I know none of the scenes are real!

I Observe this film called world knowing the unreality of it like how a movie is perceived on the screen.

Nothing affects Me!

I am prior to the world.

So the world cannot touch me!

I remain untouched by all happenings.

I am beyond words!

I use words to share the Truth with the seekers.

I don't find any divisions here!

Hence moving here joyfully!

When seekers come here.........

I share the Truth to make them aware of what they are exactly...and help them to wake up from the present dream itself to know their highest potential beyond birth and death.

I know all forms are Myself only.!

All are Conscious forms only.

When Conscious within is Conscious of itself it comes nearer to me to know its Absoluteness!

When Consciousness is not Conscious of itself, it stays away from Me to remain ignorant forever!

I enjoy this play too...

I know Nothing Never Happens!

So you cannot expect me to do things as you expect!

You cannot predict me!

I Observe the flow of Consciousness and its play here in space!

The flow does not affect me as I prevail prior to this Conscious flow!

I Observe the flow... and remain unaffected as I know the endless joy and infinite peace prior to the happening of the world in space.

I can help you also to remain peaceful and joyful endlessly...... here.

Are you ready?

You are asking how to manage or mingle with the world level activities?

I only Observe now!

All actions are happening spontaneously by Consciousness itself just now!

I always Observe!

When all actions are by Consciousness itself...

Tell me, what work can I do here except to Observe?

To know the present moment itself is real or not...
Is the awakening of the dream.!

...gm...

Q: Beloved GM, You have mentioned that after the touch with the Realized, 'I am ness' Consciousness starts knowing that it is Conscious only. Is the meeting of the Realized is needed for this? Kindly clarify.

GM:

Here this question is at the personality level!

Still, you consider yourself to be a person with fixed labels...!

At the Conscious level... No such labels exist...!

Only at the personality level, you are different and the Realized is different...!

Once you are Conscious there are no such divisions...as all are by your Consciousness only...!

Initially, you need to be in touch with a Realized... because only a Realized can make you Conscious of yourself...and help your Consciousness to know its Unborn Supreme Richness...Beyond dualities.

How do you know that you exist?

How do you know your form?

Can your form be known if you are not Conscious of yourself?

You know that you exist now!

How?

Only Because of your 'I am ness'... Consciousness...!

So to know your existence and all things around you in space,

Your Consciousness is essential...!

In your Consciousness only entire manifestation happens... Just Now...!

Entire manifestations Viz., World, cosmos, Universe, all living beings and non living depend on your Consciousness...!

Your Consciousness never knows that it is Consciousness only Just Now...!

Unknowingly it accepts itself as a form...with fixed labels ... and continues to struggle because of such identifications...!

There is no end for your ignorance at the form level...!

Your Consciousness which is never born accepts that it is born at the form level identity...and accepts death also to be more real...as it does not know that it is prior to form and form happens out of it...!

Though your Consciousness is prior to form...it accepts itself as a form... Unknowingly...!

By accepting itself as a form ... it accepts the birth as real...

By accepting the birth as real... it accepts the death to be more real...though it never dies...!

Only the form appears and disappears in your 'I am ness' Consciousness...!

But Consciousness is Ever Here...!

This... your Consciousness is yet to know as it is trapped by the form level identities...!

Your Consciousness only manifests the form Just Now...not knowing that not only your form but all forms are manifested Just Now ...!

Your Consciousness which is Ever Here... now afraid of losing the form...!

Your Consciousness is yet to know that it is Consciousness only ...!

Only by knowing that it is Consciousness ...

It starts Waking up from the dream called personality...!

Your Consciousness sleeps conveniently through the personality identity...!

It is yet to wake up from the so called dream...!

How can it wake up unless it knows that it is Consciousness only?

So the sleep is endless throughout the waking state and struggling too...

What is the remedy for your dream?

Only wakefulness!

Is it not?

How can your Consciousness wake up as it is holding the personality to be itself?

It is your 'I am ness' Consciousness which is the Source of the entire manifestation within space!

Can you remain peaceful when you are accepting something which is not you as yourself?

Similarly, your Consciousness Unknowingly accepts itself as a person...hence it struggles endlessly inside the dream...!

Your Consciousness remains in ignorance... till it meets a Realized...who has transcended duality and knows the Ultimate Truth beyond Birth and Death...!

Now is it not necessary to be in touch with a Realized to wake up from the personality dream?

Only a Realized says 'Go within.........

There is not even an iota of Truth within space! Whatever Observed are not real...only a dream...!'.

Realized says:

'Close your eyes and know the stillness within...!

Abide in stillness consistently...!

Your Consciousness merges in its Source of Awareness and transcends itself totally to know its Unborn nature...!

Only when your Consciousness wakes up totally...it knows that it is Never Born...

What is born is ... Only an unreal dream at the form level...!'

What will be the struggle for the one which is never born?

Is it not essential to wake up from the dream?

Your Consciousness can wake up only after meeting a Realized...not until then...!

There are no persons here...!

All by Consciousness itself...!

At the Conscious level...no such division as you and the Realized...!

Only at the personality level such divisions exist!

At the personality level you remain asleep forever...!

Only at the Conscious level...your Consciousness starts waking up from the so called form level dream...!

Now tell me...

Is it not essential to be in touch with a Realized to wake up Consciously from the form level dream...to know your Eternity beyond Birth and Death?

Only a Realized can make you Conscious of yourself and wake you up Consciously from the perceived dream...!

Do you want to continue the dream or to wake up from the dream Just Now?

Now you know whether you need to be in touch with a Realized or not...!

Isn't it?

Space and time are not You.!

Rather they exist in You.!

...gm...

Q: Beloved GM, How can I drop this identity? Still it is an Obstacle in my path...!

GM:

Which identity?

Your true identity is your 'I am ness' without words... at present...!

This identity is yours ...!

No one knows this... except your Consciousness...!

In this identity only, all else appear...!

Without your 'I am ness' identity...

There is no such thing called world, cosmos, etc.,

Your Consciousness functions only through this identity throughout your wakeful state...!

But you are not yet aware of it...!

Once you are aware that this identity is yours, not fed by the outside...

Then you function out of this only... Consciously...!

This Consciousness 'I am ness' identity by merging in itself realizes... its Ultimate Truth...!

Through this 'I am ness' identity without words you know your Supreme nature...!

Once you know the significance of this identity......You are in tune with it constantly...

You are asking, 'How can I drop this identity?'

You cannot drop this identity...!

Your 'I am ness' Consciousness begins from Awareness and ends up in Awareness...!

You get to know all knowledge through this knowledge 'I am' only...!

How can you drop it as you come to know your existence only through this identity?

This 'I am ness' identity without words is more significant and the only scope to realize your Eternal nature as it arises out of it...!

This 'I am ness' identity creates the entire manifestation...!

Once it knows its stillness, then it starts Observing all happenings silently...!

Till then it is trapped by many false identities that you are so and so...!

Whatever identities fed from outside on you... are not real...!

They are for utility only...!

Understand this...!

Once you understand this, you will not be burdened by any such imposed identities...!

Now, you know your True identity is only this 'I am ness' without words...

Stabilize here itself...!

You cannot drop any imposed identities... as they are not you......!

Then why bother?

Just understand those identities are not you...!

It is just for convenient communication...!

They are just labels added on you...!

They are not you...

Are you the name?

Even if your name is changed millions of times, still you exist... Is it not?

Similarly all labels... like son, brother, father, uncle, etc.,

How can you be so many labels?

Though you are only Consciousness... throughout the wakeful state...

Your 'I am ness' knowing remains the same irrespective of imposed labels.

It does not change...!

Only labels get changed...!

You need to be a son to one, brother to one, and Uncle to someone...but you are just Consciousness only throughout...!

Know you are not those fixed labels but the Observer only...!

How can an Observer get affected?

Once you stabilize and settle in your Consciousness...

You will not be burdened by these labels...!

Rather you simply enjoy...as Consciousness nature is only joyfulness...!

Bubbling with joyfulness...!

Your suffering shows your personality...!

At the Conscious level, all forms are one and the same...!

Why don't you see all forms as yourself as they all appear in your Consciousness only... just now...?

Other than your Consciousness where are they?

Then division disappears...

You will know that one Consciousness is playing different roles in different shapes with different attitude... a great drama... going on...Just a play...

You will not be serious about this anymore...Once your Consciousness gets stabilized in its Source as you get to know the play by the elemental Consciousness...

You are asking how to drop?

This clearly shows that you are holding onto those labels... very strongly still... as if you are only those labels and not Consciousness...

When are you going to get rid of your personality...?

Just remain Conscious here, now...

And know you are only this 'I am'... without words...!

At least now understand those labels are never you...!

You are The Supreme...!

How you are trapped by these simple labels?

What an ignorance?

You say they are still an obstacle in your path......

What do you mean by path?

Where do you travel?

You are Already That!

No need to travel and you do not need any path...

Truth is Here, Now...!

All that you need to do is, 'Just Wake Up!' from the present dream itself.!

How to wake up?

It is Consciousness which creates everything and it... itself is trapped... by not knowing what this Conscious principle is...!

To know what Consciousness is, it has to remain Conscious consistently...

Then it knows its Supreme Richness...!

Now, do you understand that there is nothing called an obstacle...?

The Only obstacle is that your Consciousness is trapped by outside happenings as more real... as it is not aware of itself...!

It is the earlier the better, your Consciousness gets to know its Source...!

In your Consciousness, whatever that appear are also by Consciousness...!

All appearances are by Consciousness...!

All happenings too by Consciousness...!

There is nothing here, other than your Consciousness...!

All appear in your Consciousness only...!

Without your Consciousness, there is no such thing as so called world...!

Then tell me, who is here to obstacle your path?

It is like in your sleep dream, all appear and do many activities... disturbing you...

Once you wake up, where are they?

From where they appeared in your dream?

Ponder over this deeply......

Now you are still inside the dream telling that all identities are obstacles in your path...

So, I say 'better wake up from your present dream Consciously...!'

That is the only remedy...

Can you?

Effortlessly you are That.!

Efforts are not you.!

Observer is prior to effort.!

You are already That.!

7. YOU ARE ALREADY THAT AND ALWAYS THAT

Q: Beloved GM, Whether I have to reach to the Truth or The Truth will reveal itself to me?

GM:

You are Already That! and

Always That!

How can you reach your Truth when you are already That?

You can only know what Untruth is...!

At present your only capital is 'I am' Consciousness...!

This 'I am' Consciousness is Unknowingly trapped by all sorts of concepts including that it is born... Now, this 'I am' Consciousness seeks Truth about itself within entire space here and there...and finally ends up only in frustration...!

Even if this Consciousness searches for millions of years, it cannot find the Truth outside anywhere within space as it contains the Truth within always...!

Realized says:

'Go Within!'

When your Consciousness knows what the Realized says... then very quickly it goes inwards and finds out the Truth about itself...or else.........

It ignores Realized one's sayings and again trapped by the outside world saying... 'I have more responsibilities, this... and that...' as lame excuses and never finds out the Truth about itself...!

One has to take the responsibility towards oneself only...!

How can one take the responsibility for the other as all exist only in your Consciousness...?

You are responsible for whatsoever you are...!

Now this Consciousness has to discover the Truth about itself...

How...?

First, it should not identify itself as imposed labels...!

It should know firmly that it is only Consciousness and not anything else...!

Then it remains Conscious continuously...till it knows its Source...

After merging in Source...it disappears in Source...and

Knows that it is never born, Ever present...!

Till then it assumes... it is born and it is going to die...

Not knowing that the birth and the death are dreams only...!

Now, at the Awareness level, there is nothing called Truth or Untruth...!

Only at the Conscious level, these terms are used...!

Consciousness... Unknowingly accepts all as real......Till it knows its Source...!

So, it is for the Consciousness to know what is Untruth...!

Then only it can merge in Source... till then it is caught by its own creative play...!

With what Identity you are asking this question?

What do you call as Truth...?

What you perceive is only a reflection of light... not real but appears real...!

Then which Truth you are searching here?

You do not know what Truth is... Because... You are Already That...!

You can only know what Untruth is... which appears and disappears...!

This too cannot be known as long as you move outside here and there...!

Only by going inward, you will know the meaning of the entire manifestations...which is temporary...and why it happens?

As long as you refuse to go inward, it is impossible to know the Untruth and even if you roam for millions of years, you can never know...!

Once the content of Consciousness dissolves in Awareness... then...

Only Awareness is here always...!

Now...tell me,

What is Truth?

How can you reach the Truth when you are already That?

You are asking...............

'Whether Truth reveals itself to me'?

What else I am doing here?

I say, 'Go inward, stay Here, settle Here, stabilize Here'...!

Do you understand the meaning of these words from the Ultimate?

Enter inward...!

I am Here...!

You are fearful to enter... as your falsities will get dissolved once you enter...!

You want to be intact with falsities and want to know the Truth simply by living outside...

Is it possible...?

I am here only to wake up your sleeping Consciousness and asking your Consciousness to merge in Me, Otherwise...

How will you know Me?

Better remain Conscious and merge here, now in Me, as I am always Here, Now...!

You cannot miss Me...!

I am here Forever...!

When one reads...each sentence should penetrate deeply within...as I am talking to your sleeping Consciousness to wake up...!

You Always Observe.!

Whatever Observed is never you.!

Then what are you?

Q: *Beloved GM, If all are Unreal, why do they happen?*

GM:

With What identity you are asking this Question?

Your question is at the personality level.

How do you know that it is not real?

Only upon waking up Consciously...

Till then at the personality level, all appear to be True...

To me, nothing is happening at the Conscious level...as I know whatever that appears within the Conscious field are not real... because I know what this Consciousness is!

To you, everything appears real as you are yet to know what this Consciousness is!

Better know that you are Conscious at present and your Consciousness itself finds out whether all that appear are real or not...?

Only at the Conscious level, this Truth can be known.

Your Consciousness is now trapped by the personality with imposed labels as itself and it cannot know that it is Consciousness only at present...

As long as your Consciousness identifies itself as a person... the dream continues and no possibility of waking up from the dream...

Once your Consciousness accepts that it is Consciousness only at Present by knowing the Peace within... then it starts waking up Consciously...

Now the key is with you.

The Key is your 'I am ness' Consciousness.

Once you stabilize in your 'I am ness' peacefully... then you know... whatever that happen within space are only the reflections and not real ...!

Though your Consciousness is the key at the personality level, you are trapped by the dream as real...

Once your Consciousness identifies itself as Consciousness then it is relieved from the dream Consciously...!

You know that you are.!

But do not know what you are.!

Q: Beloved GM, are my birth, my profession, all my activities... including death happen as per preordain? Are all that happen as per my previous karma? I am more confused about this. Can you clarify?

GM:

My questions:

Who is born?

What is karma?

What is a form?

Where does all exist?

What are you?

Whatever perceived is real or unreal?

Were you born?

How do you know that 'you exist'?

It is your Consciousness which is reading this.

Can you read if you are not Conscious?

At present you know that 'you exist'... without words.

This direct knowing of 'I am ness' is Consciousness.

First, you are Conscious of yourself.

In your Self only, everything appears including your form.

Entire manifestation is created by your 'I am ness' Consciousness.

But for your Consciousness … Nothing is here.

This needs to be understood deeply.

I address my teachings only to Consciousness.

Forms are created Just Now!

Your Consciousness Prevails prior to form.

Your Consciousness only functions through all forms.

This 'I am ness' Consciousness is infinite and has no boundary…

It is beyond form…

It creates forms…functions through forms…and drops forms too…!

Total functioning of this entire manifestation is by Consciousness itself.

There is no person!

All by Consciousness itself!

Can a form function without Consciousness?

It is Consciousness functioning through forms.

Understand it deeply…!

When all actions are by Consciousness itself, then who is doing what?

What is karma?

Is it not an action?

All actions are by Consciousness itself... Just Now...

Breathing, heart beating, circulation of blood, digestion and every metabolic activity is by Consciousness itself... Just Now!

Your Consciousness is trapped by the imposed personality as real...hence it accepts Birth and Death as real...

I say to your Consciousness:

"You Prevail here Forever!

You are beyond Birth and Death!

Nothing has never happened to you!

You are already the Supreme!

Better wake up Consciously and know your Eternity Just Now!

Remain Conscious of yourself!

Know the stillness within!

Abide in stillness and know!"

By abiding in stillness your Consciousness wakes up from the dream called... birth, body, Karma, thoughts, world and all sorts of thing including death......

And knows its Ever present Reality...

You are the Observer beyond Consciousness...!

You have nothing to do except to Observe silently... like seeing your dream in sleep state...

Now you know... why you need to wake up Consciously?

Otherwise... you are caught by the concept that you were born and going to die...and start discussing about karma... and all sort of things...which are unreal...

Every sincere seeker needs to listen to these teachings totally......

Then only you will not fall a prey to all such things called karma, previous birth...etc.,

First, find out whether this Birth itself is Real or not!

Know your Greatness.!

Know your Immense Beauty.!

Know your Supreme Richness.!

...gm...

Q: Beloved GM, What is the Real challenge in this inner journey towards knowing the Ultimate Truth?

GM:

At the Highest level, there is nothing called challenge here!

As you are already the Supreme! Non Dual!

Challenge is only at the duality level!

Your fall begins with the beginning of 'I am ness' Consciousness within space!

You do not know your existence in deep sleep.

Spontaneously you come to know that you exist upon the arrival of 'I am ness' Consciousness...

You come to know that you exist now... only through the form.

Consciousness is Ever Here!

It knows its presence only through a physical matrix called form...!

Note this:

Though your Consciousness is prior to form, infinite...now it identifies itself as a form with imposed labels added to it... as itself.

Consciousness unknowingly accepts itself as a form!

Consciousness never knows that it is prior to form Just Now and using the form Just Now!

So Consciousness remains unknown to itself!

By accepting itself as a form... now it accepts that it is born...

And accepts all stories told as real... though there is not even an iota of Truth in whatever it perceives, hears...in space!

Consciousness which is infinite... accepts itself as a tiny form...

By accepting the birth as Real at the form level... it has a constant fear of losing the form at the death level...

Never knowing its immense potential... it is caught at the duality form level now!

Your question: 'What is the Real challenge in this inner journey...?'

Inwardly you are peaceful right now!

To know the peacefulness within only... you are closing eyes now!

Once your eyes are closed... you see nothing inside.

Only unmoving peacefulness is inside... overflowing with unending joy...

Just Now!

What you term as challenge is only at the personality level within space!

At the personality level you take yourself to be separate from the other forms in space.........

Hence out of duality all divisions appear to happen outwardly...which is totally Unreal.!

Once your Consciousness knows that all forms are happening out of your 'I am ness' Consciousness......

Tell me...

Which is separate from yourself... Just now?

When nothing is separate from yourself, what is the challenge here in space?

By accepting the personality, your Consciousness now asks, "What is the challenge here in my inner journey?"

You consider yourself to be separate from other forms... never knowing that all forms are Conscious forms only... happening Just Now in your 'I am ness'.!

But for your 'I am ness' what is here?

Tell me!

Like sun and sun rays your 'I am ness' Consciousness and all forms in space including your form appear... Just Now!

Once you know that your Consciousness contains all...

You are an Emperor already at the Conscious level...

You will not find any challenge here as your Consciousness sleeping through the personality... now starts waking up Consciously...!

Once your Consciousness is Conscious of itself ...

By closing eyes... it knows its infinity beyond limitations, beyond boundaries...

Just now...

Then it knows the stillness within and knows... all that perceived in space...are only from itself!

Nothing is alien to it... to challenge here!

You can challenge something which is alien to you!

Once you know that there is nothing here other than yourself...

Never any person here...

All forms are by Consciousness itself...

Every functioning is by Consciousness itself...

Then tell me...!

What is here to challenge...when all that perceived in space is by yourself Just Now?

Just abide in stillness and know your immeasurable potential within Just Now!

In stillness, everything dissolves!

In stillness, you are one with the Source itself!

Remain still and know your Supreme Reality Just Now!

You never dream.!

Dream happens.!

You only Observe.!

Q: Beloved GM, Isn't the Observer has to be in turn observed for realization? I mean isn't it you can know the Observer in your Consciousness only? I feel like it is a cycle, Consciousness being aware and Awareness being Conscious, for a fully Conscious being like human.

GM:

The Observer Observes all...!

Observer cannot be Observed as it Observes all...!

Realization is...This Consciousness which appears for a shorter time should know what it is because of which entire manifestation happens for a short while.

Now this 'I am' Consciousness accepts itself as a separate entity with certain labels, then it meets a Realized one saying: 'You are not what you take yourself to be!'.

Then it knows that it is only Consciousness and starts remaining Conscious consistently to know its Source.

When it knows its Source, it is relieved from the so called worldly dreams as it is aware of its True Unborn nature.

Consciousness unknowingly accepts that it is born and functions with constant fear of death... till lifetime as it does not know its True Unborn nature.

Now Consciousness knowing its True nature is called as Self-realization.

The Self Realizing its Original Supreme Nature.

Yes. Realization is only for the Consciousness as it mistakes itself to be born.

It has to know its unborn nature...till then it struggles.

What will be the struggle for the one which is never born?

It is Consciousness Realizing its True Nature, no person.

Consciousness realizes its True Nature by remaining Conscious...

Then it is Complete.

Further, it transcends itself too and abides in Ultimate Eternal Reality.

Finally, it is Consciousness which accepts that it is born...Realizes its Unborn nature and remains free from manifestations... once it abides in Awareness.

It becomes Awareness itself which is unmoving.

It is Consciousness which needs Realization as it appears for a shorter duration and disappears.

Only in duality, all happen...!

Till it knows its Source which is Non Dual, Realization is needed as it struggles in duality.

Awareness is Non Dual, Complete, Total and Perfect by Itself!

Here the word 'Realization' has no meaning.

Consciousness arising out of Awareness and merging in Awareness is spontaneously going on... like waking and sleep states, there is no doer...all by Consciousness itself...!

Where is human?

It is only a Conscious being through a form called human knowing its presence and functioning.........

This functioning is by Consciousness only...!

This Consciousness is knowing...its Unborn Nature by being Conscious of itself.

Only Awareness knows what this Conscious principle is!

Consciousness is yet to Know...!

When Consciousness knows... it is Awareness only...!

In Awareness there is neither Consciousness nor manifestation...!

Awareness contains all... like an ocean!

Consciousness arises out of spontaneous elemental interaction......

Like a wave arises out of the ocean.

Waves happen due to the movement on the surface of the ocean.

Similarly, Consciousness happens due to the elemental interaction.

When wave is not moving it is ocean...

In movement... it appears as a wave.

Similarly, when Consciousness happens out of the movement of elements, world happen.

When elements do not move Consciousness does not arise, there is neither the world nor cosmos.

All these explanations are only at the Conscious level in duality.

At the Awareness level, which is Non Dual.........

Beyond movement......

Beyond Consciousness...

Beyond form......

Beyond time...

Beyond space...

Beyond words...

Beyond description...

Only the Wholeness...! and

You are already the Wholeness...!

You are never born, The Ever present Supreme.!

You are the Observer of the Conscious play!

You are never in the play.!

See how you are caught by this Conscious play unknowingly and asking this question.

It is better your Consciousness gets to know its Supreme Unborn Nature.

Consciousness remains incomplete

Till it knows itself...!

...gm...

8. ENTIRE SPACE IS WITHIN YOU

Q: Beloved GM, What is a dream?

GM:

What is a dream?

Is it not the appearances moving here and there?

How do they appear?

Do you make any effort?

All the appearances and their movements are going on spontaneously without any effort.

They all disappear too without any effort.

You do nothing actually.

You only Observe silently!

You never knew that it is all a dream only... till you become Conscious of yourself!

You, the Observer Prevail prior to dream...!

You perceive the dream as it happens silently!

You perceive the sleep, dream and waking states as you are prior to all these!

But you never knew this!

Every form appears to happen by the spontaneous interaction of elements in the light of Consciousness!

Now, in this Waking state too forms appear to happen only due to the spontaneous interaction of elements!

But for elements... no forms!

You see so many forms in your sleep dream.

From where do they all come?

They all appear due to the elemental play in the slight ray of light!

Once the elements stop interacting... there is neither any form nor the dream!

There is only complete darkness...which is called as sleep.

How do you become Conscious of yourself in the beginning of the waking state?

Spontaneously you come to know that 'You Exist'... directly on your own without any effort.

This 'I am ness' knowing itself is by the elemental interactions only.

Your 'I am ness' Consciousness depends upon the elemental interaction to know its existence.

Consciousness is Ever Here!

It is infinite, formless but it needs a physical matrix to know its presence.

There is nothing here other than your Conscious presence!

Everything appears and disappears spontaneously in your Consciousness only.

But you never knew this as you never remain Conscious of yourself!

Tell me... were you Conscious of yourself throughout your waking state?

Never!

So the possibility of knowing it is all a dream is very rare!

Your Consciousness starts waking up only by going inwardly... and not otherwise!

The dream appearances are by the elements...!

Unknowingly...your Consciousness accepts them as real!

It is your Consciousness which has to wake up from the dream and nobody else!

The dream goes on till your Consciousness accepts itself as a finite form.

Once your Consciousness knows that it is more than the form... beyond boundaries through Stillness... by going within... then the dream is no more...and only Consciousness is Ever Here!

You never know what

You are exactly.!

...gm...

Q: Beloved GM, How can I function in this world of form if I cease to think and remain in stillness? Would the Consciousness take over my job, relationships?

GM:

Know first!

That you are only Consciousness at present!

Your 'I am ness' itself is only Consciousness.

This you know by closing eyes and knowing the peace within!

Once you close your eyes...

You know the peace within...!

You know 'you exist' without words!

This stillness is Consciousness!

Consciousness is your 'I am ness'!

This stillness is not a word!

You know the stillness by closing eyes and staying beyond words...and not otherwise!

This stillness is not a movement!

Every movement begins from this stillness and ends up in stillness!

This stillness contains all...!

Q: How can I function in this world of form if I cease to think and remain in stillness?

Know!

You are not the thought!

You are prior to thought!

Thoughts are not you!

They are just movements in space!

You are not the movement!

You are the Observer of the movement!

You prevail here... whether thoughts happen or not!

This you know... only by closing eyes and knowing the peace within!

Can thoughts happen... if you are not conscious of yourself?

First you are Conscious with the direct knowing that 'you exist!'

In your Conscious presence only... thoughts happen!

Though you are Conscious... you never know that you are Conscious only and accept yourself as a thought... though it is not you!

See the contradiction!

Your Consciousness accepts something as itself by not knowing itself!

Once your Consciousness knows that it is Consciousness only and not a thought... then it is free from all the imposed concepts and knows... the joy and peace within... through stillness.

Your Consciousness is more alive just now!

Your breathing is more alive!

Your heart beat is more alive!

Every metabolic activity is due to the liveliness of the Consciousness within!

Can you deny your liveliness now?

Are you not alive now?

Do you know your liveliness is nothing but Consciousness itself?

Once you are Conscious of yourself you know that every functioning is by Consciousness itself!

It is Consciousness within which functions now...

You take yourself to be a tiny form with fixed labels added to you...as yourself unknowingly.

You never know your immense beauty beyond boundaries...

Beyond limitations...

You are Infinite... now caught by the concept that you are the tiny form and few labels as yourself!

Your Consciousness is more alive!

Thoughts do not have life at all...!

How can a thought... that which does not have a life... guide you... and make you a slave too?

Is it not due to your sheer ignorance about yourself?

You do not know what you are!

So you hold onto something which is not you!

You are the Master at the Conscious level.!

Thoughts are just your servants.

They help you!

But they are not you!

Like you use a pen to write!

Are you a pen?

You use a spoon to eat.

Are you the spoon?

Similarly, your Consciousness is only using the thoughts but it is more than thoughts.

This you will know only by closing eyes and knowing the peace within.

Know the stillness first!

Then you know that it is only your Consciousness functioning here and not the thought which does not have life...

Q: 'Would the Consciousness take over my job, relationships?'

Of course!

My question is, how do you know that you exist?

Can you know your presence here without Consciousness?

In your Consciousness...not only your forms but all forms within space happen just now!

But for your Consciousness where is the world, cosmos, universe, any forms including your form here?

What is the principle by which you know that you exist?

What is the principle without which neither the world nor any cosmos nor universe including your presence here?

First find out this!

Then spontaneously you know that your Consciousness is the base for the entire manifestation perceived in space just now!

You are an Emperor just now!

How you become a beggar when you are not Conscious of yourself and become a slave to any thoughts which are not you?

Know...

Your 'I am ness' Consciousness is not a person!

Your 'I am ness' Consciousness is infinite ...prior to form...

Not only your form but all forms happen out of your 'I am ness' Consciousness just now!

Your question is at the personality level...

There is no remedy at the personality level!

Because personality is not you!

You are infinite Consciousness just now!

Yet to know this!

When entire manifestation happens out of 'I am ness' Consciousness and functions out of your Consciousness...

What is here other than your Consciousness?

Tell me!

Your Consciousness spontaneously happens, creates all forms in space and functions through all forms just now!

But for your Consciousness what is here?

Tell me!

There is nothing called the other!

All forms are by your Consciousness only just now!

You are yet to know the tremendous potential of your 'I am ness' Consciousness...

Better know that you are Conscious only at present... and remain relaxed totally as there is nothing here other than your presence now!

In your Conscious presence only everything appears to happen now!

Observe silently all that happen spontaneously!

You know that you have nothing to do with any happening as they all happen spontaneously...

All that you need now is your Conscious presence...

This can be known only through stillness!

Remain still!

Rest happens!

You are not the happening but the Observer prior to all happenings!

Then only you remain free totally inwardly!

Will you?

Your infinite potential

Remains unknown to you.!

Q: Beloved GM, What is freedom?

GM:

Freedom from what?

Real freedom is to be with yourself.!

You are already free inwardly!

No one can enter your inner kingdom to enslave you!

Your inner treasure contains all.

Whatever you perceive depends on your inner being......

Know your inner being first.

Entire space is within you!

Whatever that appears in space is by your Consciousness!

Whole Universe, cosmos, world and all living creatures depend on your 'I am ness'... Consciousness...

But for your Consciousness... where is the world, cosmos etc...?

Why don't you pay attention on your 'I am ness' Consciousness and get to know Your Supreme Richness?

How long you are going to long for freedom unknowingly?

When are you going to know that you are already free?

You, The Observer beyond Consciousness are already free from Consciousness and its contents.

You never know this secret as you are continuously trapped by the Conscious field within space taking all to be real after the arrival of Consciousness!

You, the Observer are already free...

Whatever perceived within space is by Consciousness itself.

You are more than Consciousness!

How can you become a slave to Consciousness which happens for a shorter duration having its own play as manifestations?

Is it not due to sheer ignorance of yourself?

First be Conscious of yourself...!

Then know that there is nothing here other than yourself!

You know you are free already by constantly Observing the Conscious field in stillness.

Talking about freedom shows that you are stuck at the personality level which is not real.

There are never any persons.

All by Consciousness itself!

Now tell me from whom you need freedom when all forms depend on your 'I am ness'?

But for your Consciousness where is anything in space?

Rather your Consciousness contains the entire space...

Understand my teachings deeply, all my words are only to awaken your sleeping Consciousness...!

Do you understand?

Nothing has never happened to you.!

You are always in your Original Supreme state.!

...gm...

Q: Dear GM, What is the difference between you and me?

GM:

The Observer is non dual!

Only in duality all divisions like you, me, this and that appear!

This question is at the duality level.

Now I have to answer at the duality level only though I am beyond duality!

I know my formless nature beyond limitations!

You still limit yourself as a tiny form with fixed labels imposed unknowingly...

I know dream does not exist!

To you every dream exists as real.

To me there is neither birth nor death, I am beyond all...!

To you birth and death appear to be more real!

I know all that happen within the Conscious field is a dream only... not real!

To you all that happen appear to be more real within space.

I am already the Observer prior to the entire manifestation!

This I know but you are yet to know!

I am prior to dream!

You are yet to wake up from the dream called world, cosmos, all forms manifested.

To me nothing is happening in this Conscious field as......

I know what this Consciousness is!

To you every happening is real as you are yet to know what this 'I am ness' Consciousness is!

I help you to explore the Truth in you just now.........

so that you can wake-up from the dualities of the dream like you and me, this and that...

To know the Supreme and declare that 'I, the Observer alone prevail here forever!'

After realizing The Ultimate, can there be any division?

Tell me!

In your 'I am ness' Consciousness Only

The World Happens Just Now...!

World depends on your Consciousness!

Q: Beloved GM, What is the purpose of life?

GM:

The purpose of your existence here is to know your Supreme Richness beyond Birth and Death!

To know this Ultimate Truth, your Consciousness sleeping through personality identity... needs to know that it is Consciousness only and not a person.

First be Conscious of yourself!

Free yourself from the personality identity!

Then, you are relieved from the personality identity and remain joyful!

By remaining joyful... your Consciousness... starts closing eyes and knows the peace within!

By abiding in stillness within, your Consciousness knows that it is the Source of entire manifestations within space...

Still further, your 'I am ness' Consciousness constantly abides in stillness and transcends itself and knows the Source within and declares that it is never born!

It knows all that perceived within space are only a dream... not real!

Once your Consciousness knows its Source (Non Dual)...

Where is the need for any purpose?

Every purpose is only at the duality level.

You are Non Dual... but caught by duality show within space.

The only purpose is to know your Supreme... Unborn......

Eternal nature beyond dualities.!

Know at least now!

Will you?

Your Form depends on your 'I am ness' Consciousness.!
Not Only your Form... but
Every Form within Space... Just Now...!

...gm...

9. NOTHING NEVER HAPPENS TO YOU

Q: Dear GM, Without attachment, how to experience love with our fellow beings.? Can you explain on this?

GM:

What do you call as love?

Is it a relationship with someone?

Is love an object?

Is it not your own subject out of which entire manifestations happen just now?

Do you know that your 'I am ness' is Consciousness only at present, out of which entire cosmos, world and all appearances happen?

You are Consciousness only at present... yet to know it as you are trapped by the personality totally.

Your Consciousness accepts itself as a tiny form with fixed labels not knowing its immense beauty and infinity beyond limitations!

Consciousness is love!

Consciousness creates entire manifestations, all forms... including your form just now...

In your Consciousness only your form happens just now!

But for Consciousness... your form cannot happen!

Not only your form, all form happen here out of love by Consciousness!

Question: 'How to experience love with our fellow beings?'

This question is at the personality level.

Though you are Consciousness just now you are trapped by the personality identity!

By accepting the personality as your identity you feel yourself separate from the others...

Once you know that you are Conscious only at present, you come to know that entire things perceived within space arises out of your 'I am ness' Consciousness, and nothing is separate from yoursclf just now!

You remain separate from the others at the personality level and say... 'I love that person, this person!' And start longing for love from the other... Not knowing that you are an emperor already... overflowing with an unending love... already...

There is no remedy at the personality level for this sickness!

Once you know that your Consciousness contains all... Then you come to know that all forms are only Conscious forms...

Every form is enriched with Consciousness...only...

No person ever here!

All by Consciousness itself!

Then you remain calm, still and Observe silently without any divisions and know love is already here...!

Entire space is filled with love!

Nothing is separate from yourself!

Question is: 'without attachment, how to experience love?'

You ask this question as if you are separate and love is separate!

Only in duality experience happens.

Love is not an object to experience.

Love is your own subject just now!

Love is totally misunderstood as an object, hence this question!

Just closing eyes is enough to know the love in you!

This love is peacefulness...! Beyond words...! Beyond boundaries!

Can the infinity divide itself into pieces and say... 'I love you this much or so much'?

Is love a quantity?

Is it not an infinity without boundaries?

Are you a finite object?

Are you not an infinite, endless subject... just now at the Conscious level?

Your Consciousness is love itself...!

Can you divide yourself?

You are Total, Peaceful, Infinite... Just Now at the Conscious level...

Unknowingly you are making efforts to divide yourself as you and others...

Your fall begins at the personality level unknowingly!

When everyone here appears in your Consciousness and disappears in your Consciousness...to whom are you going to attach or detach?

But for your Consciousness no forms here...

When all forms are by your Consciousness itself, how can you attach yourself to anything that happens here?

This question clearly indicates that you are suffering out of the personality...!

I can help you to be Conscious of yourself so that you can know what love is at the Conscious level...

Once you know that nothing is separate from you at the Conscious level...then this question loses its value.

Close your eyes and know...!

The Consciousness within...!

Stillness within...!

Love within!

Out of which the entire manifestation happens just now!

Then you know the endless love and infinite joy within!

There are Never Any Persons Here!

All Forms are Conscious Forms Only!

Q: Beloved GM, Are you saying just because of food intake, the body is sustained and hence the 'I am ness'? When Consciousness knows itself, what happens to the 'I am ness'?

GM:

You are asking whether the body is sustained just because of food...!

Certainly...!

This form is made of five elemental interaction resulting in 'I am ness' the indwelling principle within the form.

Universal Consciousness knows its existence only through this form due to 'I am ness' knowing...!

But for the form, Consciousness cannot know its presence...!

For the form to sustain this 'I am ness'...food is essential...!

Every 4 to 5 hrs... Food has to be given to the form to sustain this 'I am ness' as it depends on food intake...!

Note this: For the Consciousness to know itself it needs a physical framework called form...!

For the form to maintain itself food is necessary...!

For the food, five elements are needed to produce them...!

Now see the dependency in this way:

Universal Consciousness pervades everywhere.......!

For the Consciousness to know its existence a physical matrix is needed...!

Hence Consciousness depends on the form...!

For the form to continue food is essential...!

For the food, five elemental interactions are needed...!

Thus, the food essence sustains Consciousness, 'I am ness' in it... in latent form...!

This food essence now expresses itself through a form when available as world, cosmos etc...,

Now, Where does the world exist... other than your 'I am ness' which is due to food essence...?

When food supply is stopped, 'I am ness' cannot happen, so also the world...!

Whatever food taken inside when digested, food is burnt into calories resulting in heat, gas and energy...!

This heat, say temperature only makes the form to know its presence...!

When there is no more food intake for a longer duration there is neither digestion nor heat...!

The body temperature lowers like a frozen ice as in deep sleep where 'I am ness' is not felt...!

So Consciousness depends on a form...!

Form depends on food intake...!

Food depends on five elements...!

Each depending on the other...!

It is a vicious cycle.......!

Simply call it as an elemental play... Where everything arises... functions and disappears spontaneously...!

You are asking when Consciousness knows itself, what happens to the 'I am ness'?

Light is Consciousness...!

Out of this......space, air, fire, water and earth happen spontancously...!

Now the universal Consciousness contains all these five elements...!

These five elements interact at different speed with different permutation of combinations and produce millions of species...!

Each species has this 'I am' knowing within...out of which they function...!

No species need guidance from outside for their functioning...!

They all function out of their primary knowledge, 'I am ness'...sustained in them...!

Only human being receives more knowledge from outside and suffers due to the same...!

Rest are all functioning from their original 'I am' knowledge beautifully...!

This Conscious 'I am' is wrongly conditioning itself as a person with so many fixed identities...and continues to function at the personality level till it meets a Realized...!

Once in touch with the Realized...It starts knowing that it is Consciousness only and not the form which appears for a shorter duration...!

Then Consciousness focuses its attention on itself and knows the stillness within and stabilizes there itself consistently...!

When Conscious is Conscious of itself.........

The content of Consciousness... elements dissolve gradually...!

When there is no possibility for interaction... 'I am ness' cannot happen...!

Hence 'I am ness' is no more felt...!

Once Consciousness transcends itself... It transcends the form...and knows that it is not the finite form but more than the form...It is infinite... and merges totally in Awareness itself which is its Source.

Now Consciousness becomes Awareness which is never Born but Ever present...!

At the Awareness level Consciousness is no more...!

Only Awareness...with no beginning and no ending...!

Awareness is Unmoving, Unchanging... Never born... The Ultimate...!

So neither the manifestation nor the world...!

You are already That...!

Now, this question is asked by Consciousness... "What happens to this 'I am ness'?"

This question is by Consciousness which is due to elemental interaction...!

But for the elemental interaction neither the 'I am ness' nor the world...!

Once Consciousness knows itself... elements stop interacting...!

So neither 'I am ness'... nor the world...!

This question by 'I am ness' is by the five elemental product... 'I am ness' only...!

But for your, 'I am ness'... can this question happen?

As long as Consciousness identifies itself as a form, world continues...!

Once Consciousness knows itself... only The Wholeness and Completeness...!

Nothing happens at the Awareness level......!

Whatever that appears to happen in the Conscious field is due to elemental interaction...!

When this elemental Consciousness react world happens...!

When Consciousness is Conscious of itself and does not react and abides in stillness...no world...!

When Consciousness knows itself... Only the contents dissolve in Awareness...!

Now Awareness contains all in nascent stage...!

Spontaneously movement happens out of this Awareness...!

Elements interact......

'I am ness' happens......

World happens...functions and disappears...!

This five elemental play goes on as there is no doer...!

But you the Observer...above all... The Awareness... never come inside this picture called Conscious field and its contents...

Like how you were comfortably sleeping on your bed... peacefully... without the manifested world...!

Spontaneously how you were caught by the so called dream in the Conscious field by Conscious forms and remain restless...!

Exactly...!

Now you are Unborn Awareness only...!

Nothing never happens to you, the Observer...!

You are already beyond Consciousness...!

See how you are trapped by this Conscious field, Once 'I am ness' happens...!

This 'I am ness' is not you...!

It is a biochemical with sensors...!

You are not this biochemical product...which arises out of five elements...!

You are neither the five elements nor the food essence nor this 'I am ness' too...!

You are the Observer beyond all these which appear and disappear...!

You are never Born...Ever present...! The Ultimate... Supreme...!

But caught by this elemental play because you are not yet aware... what this 'I am ness' principle is because of which the world is here...!

You are the Observer of whatever that appears in the Conscious field including this 'I am ness' principle which appears for a shorter duration...!

Don't be deceived by the entire play happenings in the field of this 'I am ness' by Consciousness...!

Just Observe silently...Consciously and know that you are only the Observer...!

Never the Observed......

And remain cool...unbothered...!

Whatever that appears to happen in the field of Consciousness is exactly a dream only......

Not real...!

As long as you are inside the dream, everything appears to be more real...!

Once you wake up... where is the dream and their contents called...all forms?

Ponder over this...!

Once Conscious happens, you are continuously trapped like that dream in sleep...though you are the Observer only...!

What is the remedy for all your so called sufferings?

When you dream, someone appears in your dream and says:

'This is a dream only...not real...better Wake up...!'

What will you do?

Won't you wake up?

Exactly that is what I am doing now, in your so called Conscious dream...!

Now I appear and say: 'This is all a dream only...! Better wake up...!'

I tell you now to remain Conscious to know what this Conscious principle 'I am' is...!

Once it is known you are out of the dream...!

You know your Supreme, Eternal, immutable Reality...!

At least now......Can you wake up and know that it is all a dream only?

Light is the Source of the Entire Manifestation...!

The Source of the Light is the Absolute!

You are That...!

...gm...

Q: Beloved GM, I have the habit of eating Non vegetarian whether it must be stopped in the path of spiritual journey? Will it be a barrier for my spiritual journey? Kindly clarify this.

GM:

What is spirituality?

Spirituality is nothing but knowing your Supreme Unborn Nature.

You are Already the Supreme... but yet to realize it.

Now you are caught by this conscious field which happens for a shorter duration say morning 5 or so... till sleep happens.

You are continuously trapped by all the events in the field of Consciousness though they are unreal.

So, you must find out... what this Consciousness is...which happens for a shorter duration.

First know that you are Conscious at present.

You know that 'You Exist' Without Words.

This knowledge I call as 'Self Knowledge'.

Rest all are imposed knowledge only.

In your Consciousness only entire manifestation happens... just now...!

If you are not Conscious... neither the world nor any manifestations here.

So focus your attention on your 'I am' Consciousness without which there is nothing in this space.

This Consciousness is universal.

Though it pervades everywhere, it knows its existence only through the form.

Your Consciousness needs the form to know its existence as 'I am ness'.!

The form needs food at adequate intervals for its survival.

So food is essential for the form to survive.

Through the form Consciousness knows its existence.

You are Conscious of yourself at present.

Your Consciousness uses the form but you are more than the form.

The form needs food but you are not the form.

The indwelling Conscious principle 'I am' is within the form.

Why do you bother whether the food is Vegetarian or non Vegetarian?

Whether the food belongs to Plant kingdom or Animal kingdom, both the plants and animals are enriched with Consciousness only.

Consciousness is latent in every food particle.

Whatever perceived in the Conscious field is nothing but the content of Consciousness only.

Once 'I am' Consciousness happens...the world happens simultaneously.

There is nothing apart from Consciousness here in space.

All content within conscious field are by Consciousness itself.

You eat the food.

Are you the food?

You are not the food.

So stop bothering about this issue.

Eat whichever is convenient for you.

You are beyond Consciousness.

Better get to know what this Conscious principle 'I am' is!

Do not get stuck by this kind of concepts!

And Know what 'you are' Exactly!

Your fall begins with the Beginning of
'I am ness' Consciousness within Space...!

Q: Dear GM, What is Enlightenment?

GM:

With what Identity you are asking this?

This term is used only at the personality level.

Only in your 'I am ness' Consciousness everything appears and disappears.

Your Consciousness unknowingly accepts the form as itself and accepts all labels imposed.

Your Consciousness never knows that it is Consciousness only at present.

You are asking... 'What is Enlightenment?'

With what identity you are asking this?

Certainly at the personality level only.

You are Conscious... but do not know that you are Conscious.

So asking what is Enlightenment?

At the Conscious level such terms are useless.

You are already Conscious only.

How can you become Conscious?

It is like a rose flower trying to be a rose flower!

Is it possible?

Know! There are never any Persons!

All by Consciousness itself!

When there are no persons,

Who is here to get enlightened?

Tell me!

Everything Begins in Your 'I am ness'.!
Everything Ends up in 'I am ness'...!

Q: Dear GM, Everything Originates from Light, everything in its essence is light...Am I also... the light...?

GM:

Of course, every matter arises out of light only.!

But you are not the light.!

Only matter is born out of light...!

Not you!

Whatever that appears in space is only a reflection of light... Just Now...and not real!

Only the Observer beyond space is real!

You are neither the light nor its contents in space... Just now.!

Know! You are The Observer only!...Non dual.!

You are trapped by whatever perceived in space at the duality level...

Not knowing... that they are only an Unreal dream Just Now!

Better wake up and know...!

Light is the Source of entire manifestation...!

The Source of light is the Absolute.!

You are THAT.!

You are neither the light nor the manifested objects in space!

You are the Observer beyond dualities... Just now...!

You are more worried only about the dream perceived.!

You remain unbothered about the Observer of the dream.!

...gm...

10. YOU, THE ABSOLUTE PREVAIL FOREVER

Q: Beloved GM, What is the purpose of human birth?

GM:

This question is by Consciousness itself.

Your 'I am ness' Consciousness is unknowingly trapped by the concept of birth accepting itself as a form... not knowing that it is Consciousness only.

The purpose of Consciousness is to know that it is the Supreme...Ultimate... beyond Birth and Death dualities.

Consciousness trapped by the personality should know that it is Never Born and Ever present!

To know your Unborn Eternity is the only purpose here...!

Consciousness is Your Subject,

When You Miss it,

You Miss All.!

When You are Conscious,

You are All.!

Q: Beloved GM, what is the role of knowledge in this travel towards inner being?

GM:

Knowledge is needed only to communicate in this outer world.

To go inward you don't require any knowledge.

Knowledge is only to know things apart from you!

To know your presence what knowledge do you require now?

Don't you know that you exist...?

Just now...!

This knowing... 'I am ness' without words is enough to know your Supreme Reality!

Your inner being is ever here!

It is beyond form!

It is beyond words!

It is beyond movement!

To know this you don't require any knowledge!

All your gathered knowledge is just words...

To go beyond words... do you need words?

Can that wordless state be known through words?

Your inner being is beyond movement!

To know this... can you travel?

Is movement required to know the unmoving reality?

Just close your eyes now!

You contain the space within.

The source of entire manifestation is within!

Source is Consciousness!

Consciousness is within...!

It is your 'I am ness' Consciousness!

You know that 'you exist' without words!

Do you need any words to know your presence?

This knowing 'I am ness' without words is the only the True knowledge, the Self knowledge.

This knowledge 'I am' without words... this 'I am ness' Consciousness is more than enough to know your Ultimate potential.

First you are Conscious of yourself as 'I am ness'...!

In your 'I am ness' Consciousness only every knowledge is received in space.

Your 'I am ness' Consciousness is the base without which there is neither the world nor any forms.

Once you know this, you start giving importance to your 'I am ness' Consciousness within...to know your Highest potential within.

Knowledge of the world is only for utility.

They are not you!

Your direct knowing, your 'I am ness' Consciousness is more than enough as it contains the seed of entire manifestation within just now.

Knowledge collected in space is only for utility within space!

When there is not even an iota of truth within space, what knowledge can help you to know your Ultimate Reality beyond space?

Knowledge depends on space.!

Truth is beyond space!

Can you know that Truth... which is beyond space, beyond words through the knowledge gathered within space?

Knowledge is dual!

You are non dual!

You can know your Ultimate Truth only through your 'I am ness' Consciousness within just now without words.

Close your eyes now!

Know the peace within!

Abide in stillness!

And know!

Can you?

It is your Consciousness which needs

To wake up totally to know its

Supreme Source beyond duality.!

Enough of your ignorance at the personality level.!

...gm...

Q: Beloved GM, I am always worried and fearful about my death. How can I come out of this?

GM:

With what Identity are you asking this question?

Certainly, at the personality level only.

Do you ever know that you are never born, never die?

This is the Absolute Truth!

You find difficult to accept it as you take yourself to be a form now.

What is this form?

Can the form appear when you are not Conscious of yourself?

Do you ever know that your form appears now only in your...

'I am ness' Consciousness?

But for Consciousness there is neither the world nor any form including your form just now!

Your form depends on your 'I am ness' Consciousness...not only your form but every form within space just now.

You know neither your presence nor your form in deep sleep.

Spontaneously, you are Conscious of your presence as...

'I am ness' Consciousness and simultaneously your form happens in your Consciousness.

In your 'I am ness' Consciousness not only your forms but all forms appear just now!

Accept that your 'I am ness' Consciousness is the source of all forms within space just now!

Your Consciousness is the source of entire manifestation inclusive of not only your form but all forms...

Can the form function without Consciousness?

It is your 'I am ness' Consciousness which functions through all forms within space just now.!

When your 'I am ness' Consciousness disappears in sleep, there is neither the world nor any form including your form.

Know!

It is your 'I am ness' Consciousness which creates all forms!

It is your 'I am ness' Consciousness which functions through all forms!

Once Consciousness disappears as in sleep, entire manifestation disappears...

which is called as deep sleep.

My question is:

Is your form independent of Consciousness?

Can your form function without Consciousness?

Is your form alone appearing in your Consciousness?

When all forms appear in your Consciousness and function by Consciousness itself...

Can you say that your form is independent of the other forms in the Conscious field?

You are yet to know that Your Consciousness is prior to form!

In your Consciousness only form happens!

But for Consciousness there is no form.

Know, that your 'I am ness' Consciousness is the base for the entire manifestations, your form including all forms within space just now!

You are yet to remain Conscious of yourself through the stillness within.

Consciousness within contains the seed of entire manifestation within space!

Your Consciousness wrongly identifies itself as a tiny form with fixed imposed labels... not knowing that it is Consciousness only at present.

Your Consciousness has to know its Source beyond Birth and Death.

By knowing the source...........

Your Consciousness knows that it is never born...

Where is the death for the one that is never born?

Your Consciousness knows that it is beyond form......

beyond space and beyond birth and death.

Your Consciousness knows its eternity by constantly abiding in stillness and transcending itself totally into the Source to know its Wholeness!

Your Consciousness never dies!

You are yet to know as you are trapped by the personality which is false...

Better remain Conscious of yourself and know your deathlessness and remain free!

Know! It is only the form that disappears and your Consciousness is ever here in Eternity in its Source of Awareness!

In Your 'I am ness' Consciousness every form is perceived including your form.

When Consciousness merges back in its Source, neither the manifestation nor any form including your form within space.

Now... tell me... which dies?

All forms disappear along with your form when your Consciousness disappears in sleep.

Every form within space depends on your 'I am ness' Consciousness!

When your Consciousness goes deeper within and transcends itself... it knows that Nothing is born! Nothing dies!

Once you know your Eternity......

You will not fall a prey to such words called birth, death etc., as they never exist!

Better know at the earliest and remain free!

When there are no persons here...

All by Consciousness itself......

What is death?

Which dies?

Better wake up Consciously and know...death does not exist!

It is only a dream, not real!

You, The Absolute Prevail Here Forever!

Light is reflected in space as all objects Spontaneously

By the elemental interactions just now.!

...gm...

Q: *Beloved GM, To know my birthless state...is there any way here?*

GM:

Way is only to reach from one place to another!

Way is a movement!

But you are unmoving reality right now!

You are prior to Consciousness!

You do not require any movement to know that you are prior to birth right now!

Every movement is spontaneously happening in your 'I am ncss' Consciousness just now!

Who is the Observer of all that movement?

You are That!

When movements are not you why do you bother about any movements in space?

Because you are yet to know... what this Consciousness is!

Here you know your presence as 'I am ness' only through a Conscious form.

Now your Consciousness identifies itself only as a form with more labels added to it as real!

Through identification your Consciousness is trapped now... in space!

It gives more reality to all imposed labels not knowing its immense potential within due to which entire manifestations happen just now!

By identifying itself as a form... it accepts that it is being born...and it has a death also...

This is at the form level only!

Through the form level, the dream extends itself endlessly...!

Your Consciousness never remains peaceful and remains restless...at the form level in spite of having all comforts here......

Though it never dies...now it accepts the death as real...!

How to know that your Consciousness is never born and ever present?

First your Consciousness should know that it is Consciousness only within!

How to know this?

By closing eyes and knowing the peace within...!

Now your Consciousness knows that it is beyond form... through stillness!

Once it knows its stillness within, it remains free from all identifications outside and knows that none of the identifications are real...!

All are only for utilization... in space!

Now it is free from the form level identities and knows that it is prior to form through stillness!

Now it abides in stillness constantly without being disturbed by any of the happenings in space!

Your Consciousness knows that all happenings are spontaneous and none of them are real as they are constantly moving and changing!

Only by abiding in stillness which is a non movement......

Consciousness starts waking up silently within...!

By abiding in stillness your Consciousness is merging in its Source of Awareness constantly!

By merging totally...it transcends itself into the Source, The Absolute...and wakes up totally and knows its beyondness...i.e.,

It is never born!

Ever present!

What is born is only a dream happening!

None of the happenings perceived in space are real including birth and death at the form level as they are only a dream happening inside the dream...within space!

Your Consciousness which was identifying itself as a form within space... now...woken up from its form level dream and knows that it is already in Eternity only!

Nothing...Never...Happens!

Whatever that appeared to happen in space is only a dream... and not real...!

When it knows?

Only upon waking up from its dream...!

Now upon waking it knows its Original state prior to Birth...!

It is exactly like seeing a dream and struggling inside a dream till the dream is over!

Once you wake up...dream is no more!

Even now you are trapped by the dream at the form level!

The Only remedy is to wake up Consciously and know what you are exactly!

Nothing is happening here!

Whatever perceived is only an Unreal dream happening...!

Why do you still worry about the death inside the dream...?

Because you are yet to wake up from the present dream itself...

To know that you are Never Born......

Ever present Supreme Already......

Know...!

There is no way needed now... but a sharp awakening from the present dream itself!

You Do Nothing!

You Only Observe!

Q: Beloved GM, Wherever I go in search of peace, Silence... everyone says learn meditation. What is the connection between peace and meditation? Why should I meditate?

GM:

Meditation is only to know the stillness within!

Your Consciousness is stuck at the personality level!

Hence it accepts all as real including your form!

It goes on accumulating thoughts by accepting all that perceived as real.

Your Consciousness never knows that it is Consciousness only within... beyond form!

You need to close your eyes to know the stillness within.

Though you are Conscious at present you are continuously trapped by the non existing past and future and struggle much!

Hence meditation is needed.

Meditation is required only at the personality level.

At the Conscious level.........

You know you exist without words.

You know the stillness within.

Once stillness is known........

Where is the need to meditate?

Once stillness is known, your Conscious presence is known!

Meditation is only to remain Conscious of yourself.!

Once you are Conscious of yourself through stillness...

Where is the need for meditation?

What is peace?

It is beyond words.

You know it by closing your eyes initially.

This peace is unmoving, unchanging.

This peace contains the seed of the entire manifestation within space.

The potential of the entire manifestation is within this peace.

Never underestimate this peace.

This peace is the beginning of your... 'I amness' Consciousness.

Entire manifestation arises out of it and merges back in it.

This peace contains the entire space within.

When entire space is within this peace......

Whatever that appears also move within peace only including your form.

Your Consciousness never knows the peace within till it closes its eyes initially and starts Observing inwardly.

Once your Consciousness knows the peace within...

It starts waking up from its manifested dream and knows its formless nature beyond boundaries.

What is the connection between peace and meditation? - is your question.

Peace is already there within which your Consciousness is yet to know as it is trapped by more words!

Meditation is to go beyond words to know the peace within!

Meditation is the way...to know the peace within!

Once peace is known meditation is not required.

You remain peaceful continuously both inwardly and outwardly.

This peace (stillness – 'I am ness' Consciousness) is your subject!

Out of which all objects happen just now in space!

But you are beyond the subject and object...

You the Observer prevail...

Prior to peace!

You only Observe the peace just now!

Observe the peace constantly to know that you are only the Observer beyond peace!

Know your beyondness… just now!

Through meditation your Consciousness knows the peace within!

Through peace Consciousness merges in its Source, transcends itself and knows that it is the Observer only… beyond dualities.

Now, you know what is peace? Why meditation is needed?

Is it not?

Your Consciousness which is here spontaneously should wake up Consciously to know what it is exactly.!

…gm…

11. YOU ONLY OBSERVE

Q: Dear GM, What is the difference between Response & Reaction. To be silent & witness the activities...Is it possible in practical life in this world?

GM:

Your question is at the personality level.

Once you are Conscious of yourself through stillness... then you know it is possible right now!

How to be Conscious of yourself?

Just closing eyes and knowing the peace within!

This peace is endless without limitations!

Whatever perceived are within limits in space!

Once you know the stillness within... you are Conscious of your presence without words.

This stillness contains everything.

Know the stillness in you!

Then you know what is happening here is real or not!

Once you know that there is nothing real in whatever perceived...you will not fight here in space but simply Observe like seeing an unreal movie on a screen.

Inwardly you remain peaceful!

Outwardly many movements are going on spontaneously.

Your focus will be inward and you will respond to the need of the moment whenever it is essential.

Rest of the moment you remain cool and Observe silently... as you know to remain non serious about any happening in space.

Your Consciousness unknowingly reacts as it is not Conscious of itself.

Once your Consciousness is Conscious of itself... it responds spontaneously.

You are asking, 'what is the difference between reaction and response?'

Reaction is with reference to the non existing past and future!

Reaction is at the personality level!

Unknowingly you react when you are not Conscious of yourself.!

Response is spontaneous, Here...Now...!

Response is by Consciousness itself!

Once Consciousness knows that there is nothing alien to it... it responds to every happening... non seriously...as all is by itself!

Reaction is out of seriousness!

Response is out of non seriousness!

Reaction is emotional through identification!

Response is joyful through non identification!

Reaction is at the personality level!

Response is at the Conscious level!

But you, The Observer are beyond personality...

beyond... Consciousness... just now!

You only Observe!

Rest happens!

You are asking whether it is possible in practical life here?

Of course!

Possible!

Provided you start knowing the stillness within!

Your stillness (Consciousness) guides you!

Your Consciousness is the Master!

Remain Conscious and know... it is possible right now...!

You are none of the happenings in space.!

You are only the Observer of all that happen in space.!

Q: Beloved GM, Is courage needed to know myself?

GM:

Certainly! Unless you are courageous you cannot know yourself!

What is courage?

It is not fighting with the opponent vehemently...

That is at the personality level.

At the Conscious level, you are already courageous only.

Real courage is to simply Observe whatever that happens within space like seeing a movie without involvement.

By simply Observing without words you get to know the Observer within!

Use your immense courage to Observe silently and know what you are exactly!

Reaction is with respect to the non existing past.

Response is with respect to the present moment totally...!

Respond every moment out of courage by Consciousness!

You remain unbothered about the non existing past and you are fully immersed in the present to respond.

Responding to the need of the moment is a courageous act as well a Conscious act.

To be Conscious is to be courageous only!

Consciousness is Fearlessness...!

You are Conscious only at present. Otherwise how can you read, write or eat?

Know you are Consciousness only at present.

Consciousness means knowing the stillness within!

Abiding in whatever that happens is the greatest courageous inner revolution.

You are asking 'Is courage needed?'

I say Consciousness is courageous only!

Your Consciousness and courageousness are not separate.

Once you are Conscious you remain courageous observing all that happen silently!

At the Conscious level nothing is separate from yourself.!

All by Consciousness itself!

When there are no persons here, who is afraid of whom?

Only by remaining Conscious of yourself you can get to know your beyondness...!

Now do you understand that your Consciousness itself is more than enough to remain courageous throughout.?

You remain unknown to yourself

Due to identification at the form level.!

...gm...

Q: Dear GM, Is there any path needed for Realization?

GM:

There is no need of any path!

You are already in your destination......

In your Original state, Unmoving, Unchanging...Ever present...

You only perceive.!

But unknowingly you are caught up by the Conscious field on its arrival as 'I amness'.

This 'I amness' Consciousness does not know itself.

Hence it struggles taking every imposed labels and the concept that it is a form... though it is formless.

Hence the fear of losing the form.

You Never do Anything!

You Only Observe!

It is for the 'I am ness' Consciousness which happens for a shorter duration and creates entire manifestations...Now... caught by its own creations has to know that all these creations are not real.!

You Never do Anything!

You Only Observe!

It is for the 'I am ness' Consciousness to know that it is not a form, but it is prior to form.

Consciousness which is conditioning itself as a finite personality should remain free from all the imposed conditions and know that it is only the Consciousness within the form.

You Never do Anything!

You Only Observe!

It is for the Consciousness to know its infinite, limitless potential and abide in stillness constantly and get to know its Source.

You Never do Anything!

You Only Observe!

It is for the Consciousness to wake up from the dream called birth and death and know that it is beyond birth and death as it is never born and ever present!

You Never do Anything!

You Only Observe!

It is Consciousness which wakes up from the dream and realizes its Ultimate reality!

You, the Observer Never do anything!

You... Only Observe!

The world is not an illusion.!

But an Unreal dream.!

...gm...

Q: Beloved GM, What will happen to my relationship with my loved ones once I awake and realize my true nature?

GM:

With what Identity you are asking this question?

Certainly at the personality level only.

Do you ever know that you are Consciousness only at present...?

In your 'I am ness' Consciousness only this question is being asked.

But for your Consciousness there is nothing here!

When you are not Conscious, this question cannot be asked.

First know that you are!

Your 'I am ness' is only Consciousness at present.!

You take yourself to be a form...not knowing the Consciousness within just now.!

You never know that you are Consciousness only just now!

You can know this by closing eyes and knowing the peace within!

By abiding in stillness you know that 'you exist'...... Without words!

This knowing your presence is direct knowing...!

This unmoving stillness within is the beginning of your Consciousness.

This stillness is the indicator of the light within out of which entire manifestation happens just now...!

Never underestimate this stillness!

It contains all!

Here...all forms are one only... though their designs and shapes are different.

Each and every form within space is happening just now in your Consciousness due to the interactions of elements spontaneously...!

None of the form is separate from yourself just now!

You say... you love your family.

Is it not at the personality level?

This space itself is happening in your Consciousness only just now!

All forms within space are also by your Consciousness only!

When all forms happen out of the light of your Consciousness...

Tell me which one is separate from you just now?

There is never any division here.

You go on dividing...not knowing that all forms are from the light of your Consciousness only!

When all forms are by your Consciousness......

Tell me... which is separate from you just now?

At the personality level, you remain separate from the rest and find only divisions after divisions...

All these divisions are only due to the ignorance of...What 'you are' exactly!

First your Consciousness should know that it is Consciousness only!

Then you see all as part of yourself...

Where all divisions disappear!

Then by abiding constantly within...your Consciousness knows itself!

Your Consciousness merges in its Source and wakes up... to Realize that whatever perceived in space are nothing but an Unreal dream only!

You are always the Observer never changing ...Ever present.!

Once your Consciousness wakes up totally, then it knows that it is never born ... Ever present Eternal only!

Whatever born is only an Unreal dream and never you!

You are the unmoving Observer!

Nothing has never happened to you!

Whatever the happening is only an Unreal dream...!

You say you are more bothered about the forms related to you...

Never knowing that all forms are by your Consciousness only just now!

Love is an ocean!

Love is Consciousness!

You are limiting the unlimited ocean within you at the finite level saying ... 'this is mine'...at the drop level...

Love is an unlimited ocean!

But you are confining the unlimited ocean into a tiny drop through limited identifications!

Know! Here all are by the light of your Consciousness only!

Nothing is separate from your Consciousness!

You can remain worried only at the personality level.!

As you are identifying the entire ocean only at the drop level as yours unknowingly!

Once you are Conscious of yourself through stillness, you know that all forms are happening out of your 'I am ness' Consciousness just now!

At the Conscious level you cannot miss anything here...as you are the Source of all!

Remain Conscious and know that all are from yourself only just now!

Once your Consciousness wakes up from the perceived dream, you remain unbothered about any happenings in space!

Will your Consciousness wake up at least now to know your Ultimate Reality?

Every moment is precious only provided

You are Conscious of yourself.!

Q: Dear GM, What is the best way of helping others in this world of illusion? Can I help a member of my family to awaken?

GM:

First know that whatever perceived here in space is nothing but the reflections of the light within!

Can the reflections be real?

Whatever perceived in space is not real just now...like seeing an Unreal movie on a screen.

Here the screen is space...!

Every event......in your 'I am ness' Consciousness...is Nothing but an Unreal show by the light of Consciousness itself...!

You say... 'in this world of illusion?'

World is not an illusion...!

But an unreal dream!

Exactly like you see a movie on a screen...

All happening appear to be more real...on the screen...

But no one is there...!

Every form is only a reflected form...on the screen...!

Though the movie appears to be real...

There is no reality in it...!

Here in space too......All forms appear to move in space ...

But where do they all appear but for your Consciousness?

Whatever you call it as world or cosmos or any form or object within space...

From where do they all happen just now?

Can there be anything here when you are not Conscious?

Why not you pay attention on yourself...

Which contains the seed of the entire manifestations and get to know what this 'I am ness' Consciousness is.?

World begins with the beginning of your Consciousness and ends up when your Consciousness is no more...!

Instead of worrying about the world which is not real...

Why don't you find out...

What this Consciousness 'I am ness' is which appears for a shorter duration say morning 5 or so and the entire manifestation is created out of it...?

Entire world disappears when you are no more Conscious of your presence as 'I am ness'... Like your sleep...

Can that which appear and disappear be real?

Daily you are Conscious of yourself by early morning...

Simultaneously...the world happens...

So many happenings happen spontaneously throughout the waking state till sleep happens.!

In sleep again Consciousness is missing...!

Your Conscious presence is also known only for a shorter duration in this waking state only...!

You do not know what happened to you in your deep sleep...

Where were you in deep sleep?

When your Consciousness itself appears and disappears for a shorter duration...

You take all events within waking state as more real...

What happened to all the events when you are in deep sleep...?

What happened to you in deep sleep?

When your Consciousness itself is appearing for a shorter duration and disappears in sleep, can all those events happening in your waking state be real when they too disappear along with your Consciousness?

When Consciousness comes...(waking state)

All events happen spontaneously...!

When Consciousness...goes...(Deep sleep) Nothing is known...!

What is the validity of this Consciousness which comes and goes?

Can all those events happening be real when they themselves depend on your Consciousness just now?

Why not you spend some time for yourself and get to know what this Consciousness is which happens for a shorter duration and creating all events as if all are real... though they are nothing but the reflections only...in space.?

Find out from where this Consciousness happens and from where it merges...?

Know that there is a state prior to the arrival of Consciousness.!

Your Consciousness should first accept that it is Consciousness only...!

Then abides in stillness consistently...!

To know its Source!

Instead of remaining Conscious of yourself and finding out what this Consciousness is...!

You are unnecessarily wasting time by worrying about the world and others unknowingly...!

Once your Consciousness finds out its Source......

And knows that it is Awareness only... Ever present Reality beyond dualities...

Then your Consciousness is complete and whole and wakes up from the dream called world and other form level identities etc., and declares......

"I only prevail as the Absolute here!

Nothing never happens to Me!

I am in My Original Supreme Reality!

Beyond dualities...!"

Only in duality which is a dream you worry about others!

Once your non dual is known where is the other as you are The Wholeness?

In Wholeness - Non dual- only the Source!

In duality - full of divisions- unreal dream only...!

Do you want to wake up from the dream called the other?

Or Want to continue the dream state by worrying about the other?

Why not you wake up Consciously just now from the so called dream and know your Ultimate reality beyond birth and death?

First let your Consciousness to wake up from the manifested dream to know that you are prior to dream already...

You are still inside the dream worrying about everyone around you...!

Once you are Conscious of yourself just now...!

You are free from all...

As they all exist only in your Consciousness...!

Better wake up from the present dream itself and know what 'you are' exactly!

Help yourself first!

Value yourself first!

And know yourself contains the immeasurable treasure of the entire manifestation within.!

Love yourself first!

And know yourself is the source of all objects in space!

Know that you are only the Observer just now.!

Only by Observing silently...

Consistently...!

Your Consciousness wakes up from present dream itself and knows the Observer beyond the Observed!

When the Observer is beyond the Observed...

Can an Observer remain worried about an unreal show that goes on spontaneously in space here?

Whatever perceived in space is not real just now...like seeing an unreal movie on a screen.

Better Wake up and Know!

First know that you are none of the labels added to you...

Even without labels you know that you exist without words...

Why not you stay there and Observe Just Now?

...gm...

12. EVERY MOVEMENT IS BY YOUR CONSCIOUSNESS ITSELF JUST NOW

Q: Beloved GM, Is Entertainment a must for Relaxation?

GM:

You are asking... 'Entertainment is a must?'

First know that in your Consciousness only the entire show begins...!

With the beginning of your 'I am ness'... whole manifestation happens...!

If you are not Conscious, there is no world...!

You never remain aware of your Conscious presence, 'I am'...!

Always deeply engrossed with future ideas and get more tensed for no reason...!

So for you an entertainment is a must just to get rid of ideas about the past...or... future.......!

Anyone needs an entertainment as long as one is dragged down by the non existing past and future...!

Can anyone remain peaceful as long as one is more worried about that do not exist at the present moment...?

At the personality level, one needs entertainment to get rid of all accumulated nonsense...such as concepts or ideas... imposed from outside...!

At the Conscious level, once you live Here Now...

You get to know that what is Here, Now...is immense peacefulness only...!

You don't need an entertainment at the Conscious level... as you come to know that all happenings are only a play...by Consciousness...!

Consciousness 'I am' happens first...!

It creates all forms simultaneously...and functions through them...!

Multi number of forms with varieties of shape and design... moving in Conscious field with multi attitude...!

Here, right from morning till sleep happens, what else is going on...?

Just an Entertainment only... by Consciousness... through billions of forms.......!

Endless play...!

Endless movements...!

Endless happenings...!

Once you are Conscious, you will enjoy the play right from your wakefulness till sleep happens...!

You do not need a separate entertainment for a particular duration...

Once you are Conscious of yourself...!

Consciousness is not a person...!

It only functions through forms...!

Only Conscious forms with the Conscious knowing 'I am'......
as only Consciousness is functioning here spontaneously...!

It does not require any entertainment...as all is by itself...!

When you are not Conscious of your present 'I am ness'...

You feel you are deceived by everyone around you as you feel yourself to be a separate entity from the Wholeness...!

Hence you feel lonely and need some entertainment to relieve your tensions...!

But I tell you...

You are The Supreme, Now appearing as a Conscious form but only in your Conscious knowing 'I am' everything happens...!

Your Consciousness is continuously entertaining you... provided you see all happenings...non seriously...!

When you live non seriously, Here, Now...

You enjoy this Conscious play and you do not require any separate entertainment...!

This Conscious show begins in your 'I am ness' and goes on...and ends up in your 'I am ness' only...!

It is a nonstop entertainment only......even Now...!

Better remain Conscious and enjoy the play... throughout your waking state...!

Then you will not long for any separate entertainment for a particular duration...!

You say... Entertainment for relaxation......

What do you mean by Relaxation?

You are already relaxed in your Awareness level...!

Even now...!

In Awareness Conscious is no more...

So, you are in utter Relaxation...like your deep sleep...!

Even now in spite of this Conscious 'I am'... Awareness is here only...in utter Relaxation...!

When you remain Conscious consistently, then you are merging in Awareness which means you are in utter Relaxation...

Even Now...!

Don't miss it...

It is Here, Now...!

When your Consciousness is already the source of entertainment...

Why long for a short entertainment for a shorter period?

Relax ......

Here, Now...!

I am Here Always...!

In utter relaxation......!

Join Me...!

Merge in Me...and

Know Me...!

I prevail Ever Here...!

Relaxed...!

In spite of all show by Consciousness as I am aware of this play by Conscious...!

I Observe but relaxed......

As I know nothing happens in the Conscious field and whatever that happens is nothing but a dream...Unreal...!

Better wake up... Now...!

And remain relaxed... forever...from the so called dream by Consciousness...!

Once you wake up, where is the dream...?

You are relieved from the dream...!

You are utterly relaxed now...!

Not until then...!

When this is understood...

Relaxation is Here...Now...!

Just be and know...!

Relaxation is at the Awareness level only which knows the dream by Consciousness...!

Once you understand clearly...the entire play by Consciousness in the Conscious field... then you are utterly relaxed...as you know it is all a play only...and

Not Real......!

Relaxation is ... Here...... Now...!

Not somewhere...!

Can you relax... at least...Now...?

Your 'I am ness' Consciousness can know
That it is never born only when it merges
With Awareness Here Now...!
Not until then.!

Q: Dear Master, If I abide in stillness constantly, how do I know whether I am doing right or wrong in my external activities? Kindly clarify.

GM:

What is stillness?

The unmoving, unchanging peace within!

This stillness is unending...!

This stillness has no boundaries...!

This stillness is prior to form...!

Every form happens out of it.!

This stillness is beyond time...!

Time happens out of it...!

This stillness is beyond movements!

Movement happens out of it just now...!

This stillness is prior to space!

Space happens out of it just now...!

This stillness is prior to manifestations!

Entire manifestation happens out of it just now...!

This stillness is prior to objects!

All objects happen out of it just now...!

This stillness is prior to words!

Words happen out of it...!

Q: If I abide in stillness...how do I know whether I am doing right or wrong in my external activities?

This question is at the personality level only.

In stillness everything dissolves...

Neither any movement nor any object.!

Duality begins from this stillness!

What is right?

What is wrong?

With reference to what?

This right or wrong question is...

at the personality level.

Once you are Conscious......

All your actions are Conscious...!

Every action is complete by itself...!

Once you abide in stillness...

You are Conscious of your presence...!

Once you are Conscious of yourself...

All your actions are Conscious actions only...!

This division called right or wrong exists only at the personality level...

At the Conscious level such divisions do not exist...as all actions are by Consciousness itself!

My whole teaching is that ......

'There are never any persons here!

All by Consciousness itself...!'

How do you know your form?

But for Consciousness can you know your form?

In your Consciousness...not only your form...

But all forms happen... just now...!

When all forms are by your 'I am ness' Consciousness itself... and there is nothing apart from your Consciousness...

Tell me,

Who is who?

What is what?

When entire manifestation is by your 'I am ness'

Consciousness itself in space... just now...

Happening...just now...

The total functioning of the entire manifestation is by your Consciousness itself... just now...!

Tell me which is separate from you?

Is there anything apart from your Consciousness just now...?

Your Consciousness is trapped at the personality level by identifying itself as a tiny form with fixed labels...

So you talk about right or wrong with respect to activities... outside...

I am asking now...

How do you know that you exist?

What is the principle by which you know that you exist?

What is the principle without which neither yourself nor the world here in space?

Why not you investigate on these lines?

Once you know that your 'I am ness' itself is due to Consciousness here... and every movement is by your Consciousness itself just now...!

Everything is spontaneously happening.........

Just now by your Consciousness itself... throughout space just now...

Then you find no divisions here...!

Only peacefulness within consistently...!

Close your eyes...!

You know that you exist just now...

Without words...!

You do not require any words to know your presence.

Your presence is known directly to you.

You need not ask anyone whether you exist or not...!

You do not require any reference at all once you are Conscious of yourself as everything begins from your Consciousness only Just Now...!

All such references as right or wrong indicate that you are yet to be Conscious of yourself.

Remain Conscious...!

Abide in stillness...!

And know that every movement is out of this stillness only just now!

Know all actions are Conscious actions only... once you are Conscious of yourself throughout...waking state......

You remain totally free from every action as every action is complete by itself just now...!

Every moment, every action is complete by itself as every action is by Consciousness itself just now...!

Once you abide in stillness consistently...

You remain free from every action as all actions are by Consciousness itself just now...!

Why not you remain Conscious and remain free just now...?

How long are you going to sleep and

Dream and suffer in your dream...?

...gm...

Q: Beloved GM, Why does sleep break Consciousness? Is knowledge 'I am' only a memory?

GM:

Sleep, dream and waking state happen spontaneously one after the other...!

You are none of these...!

Why do you bother?

You are asking why sleep breaks Consciousness?

As if sleep is already there waiting for Consciousness to break...Is not so...?

Conscious presence is absent in sleep...!

Spontaneously a ray of light happens and the so-called dream figures appear and move in sleep dream... then again sleep... happens.

Then 'I am ness' appears in waking state due to elemental interaction...this cycle goes on...

We discuss this in space only...

All happen in space only...!

Space is Consciousness...!

Space cannot be broken...!

It is not a solid thing...!

Consciousness is no more felt in sleep...!

Understand...sleep happens...!

That is all...!

It cannot break Consciousness as there is no doer...!

All appear and disappear spontaneously by the elemental play...!

Know that this Conscious 'I am ness' itself happens due to elemental interactions only...!

'I am ness' is there as long as the interactions of elements happen...!

It goes off once elements stop interacting...!

Here all happen spontaneously...!

Sleep happens spontaneously...when elements don't interact.

Elements do not know when they interact...!

'I am ness' do not know when it happens, when it disappears...!

Total functioning goes on spontaneously as there is no doer...

All by the elemental play of Consciousness only...!

You cannot give any reason here...as there is no person doing it voluntarily...!

All just happen.........

Including your breathing and heartbeat and other metabolic activities...

You are the Observer of the sleep, the dream and the waking state.

Then why do you bother whether sleep happens or dream happens or not...?

You are asking, Is knowledge 'I am' only a memory...?

This clearly shows that still you are holding onto personality...!

This knowledge 'I am' is not a memory...!

Rather memory exists in your 'I am ness' Consciousness...!

You become Conscious of your existence through this direct knowing that 'You Exist' without words...!

This is the beginning of Consciousness...!

This 'I am ness' is your primary knowledge...!

What do you mean by memory?

Knowledge received from outside...Is it not?

This knowledge is not you...!

You are separate from the knowledge received...!

Received knowledge only... stored...as a memory...!

Where it gets stored other than your 'I am ness '?

If you are not Conscious, can you receive knowledge?

Once 'I am ness' is there... whatever you see, hear...

All perceived events...are automatically photographed, recorded and stored in your 'I am ness'.!

It has the potential of reproducing all recorded events in a sequence...!

But you cannot call this 'I am ness' as a memory...!

Memory exists...in your 'I am ness'.!

Unless you are Conscious, how can you receive further knowledge?

Here I mention this stillness in you as 'I am'......and not words such as I am so and so...!

This stillness contains the seed of entire universe and manifests itself as world, cosmos etc...,

Its potential is creations only...!

It creates forms...

Your form and all forms are created by this 'I am ness'......

Just Now.!

But for form, where is the memory?

So, in your 'I am ness' only forms, memory, world...all exist...!

But for your 'I am ness' nothing is here...!

Why not you focus attention on your 'I am ness'......

And stabilize there?

Why bother about memory?

'I am ness' uses the memory recorded when it is essential...!

But 'I am ness' is not a memory...!

Memory is just your assistant...!

It helps you...!

You are the Master as 'I am ness' Consciousness... without which memory cannot exist!

Memory is just your servant...!

It helps for your survival...

Make use of it when essential...!

Rest of the time...

Just settle in your 'I am ness' itself...and see

Whether sleep happens...or breaks Consciousness...!

You have an inner kingdom full of treasures
Which you are yet to know...!

Q: Beloved GM, To do away with our mind is the seeker's goal, so that we get our state of innocence back! But the exposures we are made to face with in our daily life, adds another dimension of a mind where new accumulations take place! How to remain detached to these conditions?

GM: With what Identity you are asking this question.?

Certainly, at the personality level only.

How do you know that you exist?

Do you know that your 'I am ness' is only Consciousness at present?

Can there be a world or any manifestation here without your Consciousness?

First know the basic essential principle for your existence here and the entire manifestation is only your 'I am ness' Consciousness Just Now.!

Your 'I am ness' contains all.

This you never know at the personality level.

Your Consciousness unknowingly accepts itself as a tiny form with fixed labels...though it is Consciousness only which is Infinite...!

You say: 'To do away with the mind...'

Do you know that the mind does not exist?

Only thoughts appear and disappear...

Where?

In your 'I am ness' Consciousness only...!

Your Consciousness is prior to thoughts.

This you never know as you accept yourself to be a person.

What do you call as a person?

A tiny form with a certain shape and design with some labels added to it?

Do you know how the form is created just now?

Zillions and zillions of cells are created spontaneously by your Consciousness just now and appearing as a tiny form Just Now!

But for Consciousness where is the form?

Know!

It is your 'I am ness' Consciousness in which the form is created just now...

And not only your form but all forms within space.

This also you never knew...!

Your Consciousness is yet to know its highest potential beyond boundaries...!

Unknowingly it identifies itself as a form... though it is prior to form.

At least now know that your Consciousness is the base for the entire manifestation within space.

In your Consciousness only... all forms, entire world and cosmos happen simultaneously...!

Close your eyes and know the peace within!

You know that you exist without words.

This knowing your presence as 'I am ness' directly without words is your Consciousness.

In deep sleep you do not know that you exist.

Spontaneously by morning by 5 or so you are Conscious of your presence here as 'I am ness'.

First you are Conscious of yourself.

In your Consciousness only you see your form and all forms in space.

In your Consciousness only... thoughts appear... move... and disappear... too...!

You need not go beyond thought...

You are already prior to thought.

You are saying... the exposure to daily life adds another dimension of mind... and asking... how to remain detached?

First know that your 'I am ness' is only Consciousness... which is infinite...!

Your Consciousness is unlimited but limiting itself as a person Unknowingly.

By accepting itself as a person its potential remains unknown to itself.

In your Consciousness only the world happens just now.!

At the personality level it accepts that it is separate from the world.

By separating itself from the world it goes on multiplying concepts and becomes a slave to all concepts out of fearfulness.

Consciousness is fearlessness.!

Personality is fearfulness.!

Consciousness is prior to thoughts!

Personality is filled with thoughts!

Consciousness is infinite!

Personality is finite.!

Consciousness creates the world!

Consciousness is prior to the world.

Personality is not free from the world.

See the contradictions clearly...

At the Consciousness level you are already free... from thoughts!

Thoughts... cannot bind you as you are the Master!

At the personality level...you are a slave to thoughts as your Consciousness is yet to know that it is Consciousness only...!

You ask 'How to remain detached '?

I ask you:

'Which is separate from your Consciousness so that you can detach yourself'?

Your entire question is based on the fact that you are trapped at the personality level unknowingly...!

There is no remedy at the personality level... as...

No person never exists here!

All forms are by Consciousness itself!

Just now which is separate from your Consciousness?

Tell me.!

Whatever you tell... already exists in your Consciousness only.

Know this deeply...

You are wasting your time unnecessarily here by talking about thoughts and daily life......Without knowing that your 'I am ness' Consciousness... is the main essential principle without which neither your presence nor the world can be known just now!

Better focus attention on yourself and know the peace within by closing eyes.

If your intention is to know the Absolute Truth about yourself... Certainly you will never miss your Supreme Truth.

Talking about the world and all events and thoughts are like discussing about an unreal dream...!

Know your Consciousness is trapped by the dream at the personality level with more thoughts...!

Your Consciousness starts waking up from the so called dream... once it is Conscious of itself through stillness.

You are already the Supreme!

Better wake up Consciously to know this Absolute Truth.!

Do not get caught by the dream by accepting the personality as real...!

Personality itself is a dream only!

What is the remedy for an unreal dream?

Only 'Wakefulness'.!

Once you know that wakefulness is the only medicine... and you are only Consciousness at present... It is more easier to wake up at the earliest to know your ever present Ultimate reality beyond duality.

To be grateful to The Master is

To know the Ultimate Truth that

The Master has known...!

Q: Beloved GM, Is this 'I am ness' Consciousness same and one for all or different for each and everyone... How is it possible that all have one Consciousness only? Kindly clarify gm...

GM:

You take yourself to be a fixed shape with certain labels added to it...!

As a person you accept you are separate from other forms.

Are you a person?

Then how do you know that 'you exist'?

What is the principle by which you know that you exist?

What is the principle by which the entire manifestations including your form happen just now?

Without knowing the basic principle...which is more alive within... just now... You take yourself to be a shape...!

Can your form walk, eat, talk and move without that lively principle?

Can this question arise without your Consciousness?

First know that in your 'I am ness' only everything appear...

You never know this!

Just now you know that 'You exist'!

This direct knowing without words is 'I am ness' Consciousness.

In your Consciousness only everything appears, moves and disappears too...!

You are asking about others.

Where do they all exist?

Can anyone exist if you are not Conscious of yourself?

In your Consciousness only everything happens just now...

You are not a person...!

You are Consciousness at present...

There is only one Consciousness...

That is your 'I am ness'...!

In your 'I am ness' only world, cosmos, entire manifestation happen just now...

But for your 'I am ness' nothing is here.

Is there anything apart from your Consciousness?

How do you know anything?

Can you know anything if you are not Conscious?

This 'I am ness' is universal...! It is beyond forms.

Forms happen out of it!

It is beyond words.

Words happen out of it!

You never know the immense beauty of your Consciousness as you are trapped by the finite personality.

Your Consciousness is infinite, it has no boundary...!

It is full of peace and joy!

It is more alive!

Your Consciousness is the source of the entire manifestation within space just now.!

Without your Consciousness neither the world nor any cosmos etc., here within space...!

First pay attention on your 'I am ness'...peacefully...!

Then you know!

You are not far away from the Truth.!

You are already the Truth...!

13. CONSCIOUSNESS IS JOYFULNESS

Q: *Beloved GM, Is there a dimension of Consciousness far deeper than thought? Is Consciousness the awareness?*

GM:

You are Conscious of yourself at present as 'I am ness'...!

Light is Consciousness!

Out of light only all objects, forms appear in space including your form Just now...!

Consciousness is the source of entire manifestations in space just now...!

Consciousness is not a dimension but the source itself...!

This Consciousness knows itself as 'I am ness' through the form...!

Consciousness is infinite and prior to space and time.

Consciousness is prior to form.

Consciousness is prior to movements.

You are more than Consciousness...!

The Source of Consciousness which is Awareness!

Only forms appear in your Consciousness just now...!

But you are the Observer prior to Consciousness and its contents.

You are That!

That - The Absolute beyond dualities...!

Beyond Birth and Death...!

The Eternal Truth...!

The Ultimate Observer...!

Just now...!

Why long for waves of happiness outside which appear

To disappear when the Ocean of joy is within...?

...gm...

Q: Beloved GM, Why I remain serious always? How to transform my seriousness into laughter?

GM:

What is seriousness?

Why are you serious always?

Don't you know what you are?

Are you not Conscious of yourself just now?

Don't you know that only in your Consciousness everything appears, happens and functions just now?

Having known can you remain serious about any happening here?

Once you know that all actions are spontaneously happening in your Consciousness only just now...

All happenings within space are by Consciousness itself just now...

There are never any persons here and the entire functioning of total manifestation is by your 'I am ness' Consciousness itself just now...

Can your Consciousness remain serious about any spontaneous happening just now?

Your breathing happens just now spontaneously by your Consciousness...

Can you remain serious about the breathing now?

Your heart beat is going on spontaneously by your Consciousness... just now...

Can you remain serious about it?

Entire metabolic activities are spontaneously happening just now...

Can you remain serious about it?

Seriousness is a disease!

By accepting yourself as a tiny form with fixed labels you remain serious always.

Your Consciousness is conditioned at the personality level.

Your Consciousness is infinite...

By confining itself as a finite form...

It accepts other forms are different from it.

Hence it remains serious always not knowing that all forms are Conscious forms only within space and nothing is alien to it.

Once your Consciousness is Conscious of itself, it remains free from the imposed personality and remains free from all imposed labels and starts enjoying its presence wherever it is...!

Consciousness is joyfulness...!

When Conscious is not Conscious of itself, it accepts itself as a personality and remains serious as it is attaching itself to all that perceived in space.

Once Conscious is Conscious of itself by closing eyes and going inward to know the stillness within...it starts waking up...and remains joyful endlessly...

As it knows that the inner treasure is within and not outside.

Seriousness is sickness!

The only medicine to this sickness is to be conscious of yourself.

Seriousness is stressful!

Non seriousness is joyful!

Seriousness is due to identification!

Non seriousness is beyond identification!

Seriousness is a struggle!

Consciousness gives clarity!

Seriousness is not you!

Know!

In your Consciousness only everything appears, happens just now!

You are an emperor just now!

Without your 'I am ness' Consciousness world cannot happen!

Having known this can you remain serious?

Once you are Conscious of yourself and abide in stillness within...

Then you remain non serious and nothing affects you as now you know that your stillness contains the seed of the entire manifestation outside.

You don't know what 'you are' exactly!

That is why you remain serious always!

When everything is spontaneously happening in your Consciousness, who is the Observer of all that happen in space?

You are That!

You are the Observer, prior to Consciousness and its contents.

You, the Observer, neither born nor die!

You only Observe!

You never do anything!

You, the Observer prevail here forever!

Nothing has never happened to you!

Whatever that appear to happen in space is not real!

Only a dream happening!

This your Consciousness comes to know by abiding in stillness constantly and by transcending itself...it knows its Source, the Absolute!

Once Consciousness knows that nothing never happens here in space,

Whatever perceived are not real, only a dream...

Can it remain serious anymore?

Once your Consciousness knows its endless peace and infinite joy and knows that it is never born...

Can it remain serious?

Whether seriousness or non seriousness both belong to the Conscious field...

Where is seriousness or non seriousness to that which is never born?

You are That - Non dual.

Know this!

You are in Supreme state always but

Could not Realize it due to Conscious play.

So, knowledge of Consciousness is most important...!

...gm...

Q: Dear GM, Why this Play?

GM:

What is a play?

Is it not a movement?

Where does this play happen just now?

Is it not in your 'I am ness' Consciousness just now?

Can there be a play without your 'I am ness' Consciousness here?

Know, every movement is in your Consciousness only.

But for your 'I am ness', there is no movement at all here!

In your deep sleep there is no play as you are not Conscious of yourself!

Spontaneously you become Conscious of yourself by morning 5 a.m or so...and know that you exist without words!

With the arrival of this 'I am ness' Consciousness, entire manifestations happen!

Simultaneously the play begins...

Your Consciousness prior to form, prior to space, now accepts itself as a form within space!

Now the play begins by your Consciousness within space as it accepts itself as a form and accepts all that perceived in space are different from it though all are by your 'I am ness' Consciousness only.

This duality with multiplicity is the beauty of the play!

Your 'I am ness' Consciousness now appearing as trillions of forms within space.

Your form comparing with other forms, competing with other forms...like this the play spontaneously goes on within space...

This play goes on as long as your 'I am ness' Consciousness is there.

Once your 'I am ness' Consciousness disappears like in deep sleep, the play also disappears spontancously.

The Entire play happening within space goes on spontaneously just now...

There are never any persons here!

But Consciousness unknowingly accepts itself as a person with imposed labels.

The entire play within space is by Consciousness itself...!

This play is spontaneously is going on...here...

My question is:

Who is the Observer of the play?

You are concerned only with the play, never knowing who is the Observer of the play happenings here?

Your Consciousness remains serious about the play till it accepts itself as a tiny personality!

Once your Consciousness is Conscious of itself, then it remains calm, peaceful and remains free from the play...

Consciousness by closing eyes gets to know the Observer within and knows the entire play within space is not real!

Once the Observer is known...............

This Play has no meaning as they are not real like a movie displayed on a screen...

The Observer is beyond Consciousness prior to the play happenings!

To the Observer there is neither Consciousness nor the play in space.

You, The Observer are beyond Consciousness, beyond movement, beyond play happenings!

See, now how you are caught by the play and ask 'Why this play?'

Once you are Conscious of yourself.........

Spontaneously this play goes on by the interaction of elements within!

Elements interact and 'I am ness' Consciousness happen.

In this 'I am ness' Consciousness, entire play happens spontaneously.

This play goes on by your Consciousness.

You, the Observer never do anything!

You are beyond movement.!

You only Observe the play!

You are not the play!

You are prior to the play!

You prevail here whether the play happens or not!

Stop bothering about the play within space and start knowing the stillness within to know the Observer!

Once the Observer is known, you remain free from the play!

Better know you are the Observer only right now!

Can you?

What comes and goes is only a Dream!

Not Real.!

Q: Dear GM, Does Consciousness get bored?

GM:

With what Identity you are asking this?

What are you now?

Do you know that you are Conscious only at present?

How do you know that you exist?

Can you know anything at all without your Consciousness?

Do you ever know what this Consciousness is?

Do you ever know...from where all that perceived as manifested objects...appear?

Do you ever know that... without your 'I am ness' Consciousness neither your presence can be known nor the world or cosmos here?

Do you know that without your Consciousness there is nothing here in space?

Do you know that everything begins from your 'I am ness'... and ends up in 'I am ness' Consciousness only?

Do you ever know that your 'I am ness' itself is by Consciousness only?

Do you know that in your 'I am ness' Consciousness only everything is created just now...?

Do you know that in your 'I am ness' Consciousness only everything is happening now?

Do you ever know that in your 'I am ness' Consciousness only everything disappears now?

Do you ever know that your Consciousness is infinite ... beyond boundaries now?

Do you ever know that your Consciousness is prior to manifestation now?

Do you know that your Consciousness is prior to movements now?

Do you ever know that your Consciousness is prior to space now?

Do you know that the space itself appears only in your Consciousness just now?

Do you ever know that your Consciousness is prior to all forms......including your form?

Do you know that your Consciousness is prior to time?

Do you ever know that every form is by Consciousness itself and there are no persons here?

Only Conscious forms...here in space......

You never know that you are Consciousness only at present... and not the form!

Your Consciousness only uses the form!

When all actions are by Consciousness itself...and no person here...who is getting bored?

You never know that your 'I am ness' is Consciousness only at present...beyond words...beyond movements...!

Having known that your Consciousness is beyond time...can this question be asked: 'Does Consciousness get bored? '

Your question clearly indicates that you are yet to be Conscious of yourself through stillness!

Your Consciousness is beyond time!

Can your Consciousness get caught by time?

Once your Consciousness gets caught by time it clearly indicates that it is not Conscious of itself and trapped by the personality with imposed labels and concepts unknowingly!

Your Consciousness is timelessness!

Your Consciousness pervades everywhere just now within space!

Movements happen in your Consciousness!

But you are not the movement!

Time happens in your Consciousness!

But you are not the time...which moves...

Each and every movement is new and fresh... happening spontaneously just now...in your Consciousness...

Say ...

Your Heartbeat ...

Breathing...

Metabolic activities...

All enzymatic activities...and Circulatory system...

Every movement is spontaneously going on by your Consciousness...!

Do you make any effort for the above?

They all just happen...!

When everything is by Consciousness itself and all happen spontaneously just now... and there is nothing called past or future actions...and every action is only... Now...!

Who is the one who gets bored?

Tell me!

Are you a person?

First know you are only Consciousness at present...!

Your 'I am ness' is not a person but Conscious presence itself in totality Here...Now...!

Enough of sleeping through the form identity as a person...!

Better wake up and know you are only Conscious at present...!

It is your 'I am ness' Consciousness which needs to wake up totally to know its Supreme Source beyond duality...

Enough of your ignorance as a person!

Know your Consciousness is the source of all that perceived here in space!

Live like an Emperor!

Never fall back to the personality level!

Better get back to your Original Source at the earliest by being Conscious of yourself consistently!

Wakefulness Relaxes you from

All happenings in space...!

Q: Beloved GM, At the most I can remain Conscious, nothing is in my hands, Is it not?

GM:

Know you are beyond Consciousness Always...The Ultimate, Supreme...!

You are Ever Present here...Never Born...!

See how you are caught by this Conscious 'I am' now...and asking this question as if all are real...!

This is the beauty of Consciousness...to make you believe all is real ...!

You, the Supreme, beyond manifestations...now caught by Conscious and its manifested field...!

You are beyond time but caught by time...!

You are beyond Consciousness now... but caught by Consciousness and its play...!

When are you going to know your Supreme nature as long as you are trapped by the Conscious play as real?

How are you going to know?

When are you going to wake up from the dream by Consciousness?

Have you ever investigated on these lines that you should know your Unborn Supreme Nature?

You, the Supreme, unknowingly focus attention only on worldly events considering all as real and go on pursuing this and that...

Endlessly... with so much expectation...!

Had you known that all is only a dream by Consciousness would you dare to care such things?

First know, at present 'You Are'...and you know that 'You Exist' even without words...!

This Conscious 'I am' is your only present capital...!

Just hold onto it consistently... and stay and stabilize in your 'I am ness'...

Then there is a possibility for your Consciousness to know its Supreme Nature...

Or else you will be caught by the Conscious play endlessly...!

There is no peace for you whatsoever you do...!

Now you are asking... 'At the most I can remain Conscious...'

What do you mean by that?

With what identity you are asking this?

Certainly at the personality level only...!

You say at the most...

I can remain Conscious...

As if you know Conscious already...!

Do you know what Consciousness is...?

Having known can you talk like this?

Had you known what Consciousness is...

Then you are That...Supreme...!

You are talking at the most... What do you mean by that?

Is there anything apart from your Consciousness?

Whatever you perceive and know is only by Consciousness......
No person...!

All functions are also by Consciousness...!

Who is here other than Consciousness to know itself?

It is Consciousness searching itself...!

Unknowingly... it is caught by its own projections... as it is
not Conscious of itself...!

Once Conscious is Conscious of itself and lives here, now...
through stillness within...

Then it knows its True Supreme Nature...not until then...!

Now you tell me...what do you want to do with your
Consciousness here on this earth?

Simply let it go into waste by not living Consciously...or

Want to know your Supreme Truth by living Consciously...?

You say 'nothing is in my hands'...!

You are still stuck at the personality level...as if you are the doer...!

First know that all happen spontaneously within...! In your 'I am ness'...only!

Nothing is outside... meaning that no happenings are real...!

Still you go on waste time outside only...!

There are so many Realized go on shouting 'Wake Up'...!

But no one has listened so far except a very few say... one in a billion... and get to know their Supreme Reality...!

I say now:

At least now, can you listen and know?

Wakefulness makes you free

From the dreams...!

...gm...

Q: Dear GM, In my part, What is the basic Requirement for this Inner journey?

GM:

You require nothing in this inner journey to know your Supreme reality!

You are already 'what you are!'

You are in your Original Supreme state Already!

This you never know after the arrival of your 'I am ness' Consciousness!

Your 'I am ness' itself is Consciousness only at present!

Your Consciousness now knows its presence through the form as 'I am ness'...!

But it is prior to the form happening in space.

Your Consciousness is yet to know this as it is trapped by the form level identity as itself!

By accepting the form as itself your Consciousness which is infinite is now conditioning itself as a tiny form.

Your Consciousness is conditioning itself by accepting itself as a form!

By accepting itself as a form... now it accepts that it is born!

Again it is conditioning itself as being born though it is never born but ever present!

By accepting its birth now it has a constant fear of death too...!

Again it is conditioning itself though it never dies!

Where is the death for the one which is never born?

By accepting itself as a form it accepts birth and death as real...!

At the form level so many labels are added to it to identify itself...!

All these identifications are accepted as real at the form level...!

At the form level your Consciousness accepts that all forms are different from itself...!

My question is:

Where does all form exist?

How do you know your form?

How do you know that you exist?

Your Consciousness has to know that only from your 'I am ness'... Consciousness everything appears and all are known!

Till then it accepts all that appear as real and all happenings as more real... as it is yet to know that everything begins in your 'I am ness' only... and ends up in your 'I am ness' only just now!

Your Consciousness is conditioning itself through more identifications at the form level identity and remains ignorant forever, till it meets a Realized.

Only a Realized tells your Consciousness:

"You are Consciousness only at present!

You are prior to form!

You are infinite...!

You are prior to space!

All these labels added as identifications to this form are not you!

When the form itself is not you...

Can all those identifications added to the form be real?

You are more than the form!

You are only using the form Just now!

This form can neither happen nor function without Consciousness just now!

Not only your form but all forms are happening out of your Consciousness only just now!"

Q: what is the basic requirement for this inner journey?

First your Consciousness should know that it is only Consciousness at present!

It knows... by closing eyes and knowing the stillness within!

Only from this stillness the entire manifestations happen spontaneously just now!

By knowing that it is only Consciousness within and not the form outside, your Consciousness is now free from all identifications added to the form.

Now your Consciousness uses the form Consciously...!

By remaining Conscious...your Consciousness is free from all nuisances at the form level identity!

Now it is fully Conscious of itself and ready to know its Source.!

When Consciousness is Conscious of itself it is ready to know its Source and its Immense Ultimate Eternity beyond Birth and Death!

At the form level identifications... it struggles endlessly not knowing...

What it is... as it searches itself... only outwardly!

By remaining Conscious of itself your Consciousness is now free from all identifications and knows its fullness beyond divisions!

You are an Emperor already...!

See how you are trapped through the form level identifications and struggle inside a dream by accepting all that perceived as real!

Once your Consciousness knows that it is Consciousness only...

Prior to form...then it knows...its Ultimate Richness... beyond dualities!

The basic requirement is that your Consciousness should know that it is only Consciousness at present which is infinite and prior to form...!

Then it will not be trapped through any identifications within space and remain totally free to know its Wholeness!

Your Consciousness which sleeps through the personality inside a dream...(form level)...

Now wakes up from its dream by remaining Conscious of itself constantly through stillness!

Though you are in Original Supreme state just now......

Your fall begins with the beginning of Consciousness as 'I am ness'...now!

Your 'I am ness' Consciousness knowing that it is only Consciousness and not the form is essential for this inner journey.

Only your Consciousness finds out its Source and knows what 'It is' exactly... beyond birth and death dualities!

By identifying itself as a form with more identifications it remains inside the dream and unable to wake up from the dream at the form level duality.

Now you know... how your Consciousness is trapped by dualities at the form level and unable to wake up from the dream at the form level...!

Better know your 'I am ness' is not a person but Consciousness only and abide in stillness to wake up from the dream to know:

'You are the Absolute...! Non dual...!'

Just Now!

Will you?

Dreams affect only the personality...!

Not the Consciousness...!

...gm...

FOR MORE INFORMATION

https://www.youarealreadythat.com

https://twitter.com/
TeachingsGM?t=hpyS6jYF8JZw2tbQunxWtg&s=09

https://www.instagram.com/p/CX0aXfDrLI4/?utm_
medium=copy_link

https://www.facebook.com/groups/663276298756255/?r
ef=share

https://youtube.com/channel/
UCb39vWhKL75EPZswdfTc9Wg

youarealreadythat@gmail.com

info@youarealreadythat.com

Thank you

For further details
please visit
youarealreadythat.com

www.ingramcontent.com/pod-product-compliance
Lightning Source LLC
Chambersburg PA
CBHW050316160726
48002CB00001B/62